# THE
# LEAN
# SENSEI

# THE LEAN SENSEI

## Go See Challenge

Michael **Ballé**

Nicolas **Chartier**

Pascale **Coignet**

Sandrine **Olivencia**

Daryl **Powell**

Eivind **Reke**

Lean Enterprise Institute

Library of Congress Control Number: 2019939253
Print ISBN: 978-1-934109-57-1
ebook ISBN: 978-1-934109-59-5

Lean Enterprise Institute, Inc.
27-43 Wormwood Street, Suite 410
Boston, MA 02210 USA
(t) 617-871-2900 • (f) 617-871-2999 • lean.org

*For our kids. Through their curiosity to go, see,*

*challenge and ask why, they are our true sensei!*

# CONTENTS

# INTRODUCTION

BY DANIEL JONES

Lean thinking is the alternative business model for our age—
focused on value, learning, growth and improvement—in con-
trast to the finance driven shareholder-first business model
described by Michael Porter.[1] From observing pioneering experiments in all kinds of activities across the world we have learned
how lean fundamentally challenges traditional business thinking.

---

[1]    Elaborated in M. Ballé, D. Jones, J. Chaize and O. Fiume (2017) *The
       Lean Strategy*, McGraw Hill, New York.

We have also discovered that, behind all the tools for operational excellence and the different management system needed to support their use, lies a much deeper challenge: to develop the human potential of everyone to create a culture of accelerating continuous improvement to meet today's changing circumstances. *Learning* is at the heart of lean. Indeed, lean is more accurately described as an education system rather than a production system.

Lean Thinking emerged from and continues to be inspired by the example of Toyota; and is now being reinvented as the first truly global approach to collaboratively creating value. Toyota's lean ideas have been adopted all around the world, from industry to healthcare to digital start-ups. In the early days of exploring this system, many of us learned from ex-Toyota masters who asked bewildering questions and brutally challenged existing thinking and practice. While their behavior was certainly dramatic, it could not be described as simply teaching, consulting, mentoring or coaching. Early on someone chose the term *Sensei*, used to describe the expert masters in martial arts. The term stuck and, to the amusement of many Japanese, has become part of the language of lean. Since then we have found it hard to accurately describe their important role in transmitting lean knowledge. If we are not clear about this it is easy to misunderstand the path to lean and slip back into traditional consulting and the command and control business model.

The authors of this book are an A-team of lean pioneers from France, America, Norway and Britain who have experienced and followed the path of the Sensei. They comprise a lifelong lean author who was there at the start of the movement, the CEO of a hyper-growth digital company, a process owner in a large state-owned company, a leader in the agile community, a lean writer and consultant, and a lean practitioner and academic researcher. Whatever your role, this story will change the way you think about lean. It is frankly essential reading for those seeking to make real progress with lean.

## Sensei: Teacher, Master
## [Literally "Previous" "Life"]

### ...person born before another

Lean is a system to gain competitiveness by continuously developing people. A key, and rather mysterious, character in that is the "sensei." Neither trainer, nor coach, nor consultant, the sensei is the person who helps you grow by encouraging you to look beyond the borders of your first understanding of a situation, and to solve problems differently and discover a deeper meaning. By encouraging you to deepen your thinking, the sensei also points you toward more effective ways to act and *add* value by improving things, beyond just producing value by doing the usual work. The sensei believes that to transform processes (and others), you must first learn to transform yourself.

*Value* is what we do to help someone else solve their problem. Companies are born as we discover how to deliver cost-effective solutions to generic problems. If people like a good cup of coffee, it makes sense to open a café, with a dedicated expensive coffee machine that serves the same cup to the many people who'll come there (as well as offer a welcoming place for a relaxing time). As technology evolves, it makes sense to use technical progress to solve the same problem in innovative ways, such as offering everyone a cost-effective personal coffee-maker that is just as good as the collective one in the café, without needing capital investment. And so on.

Companies are organized to deliver such value to their customers, and through offering more and better products and services, benefit society. Companies need to make a profit to continue to help customers with existing solutions and to invest in the search for new ones. Profitability is the result of both how desirable the product is at a given time, and how well the people in the company organize themselves to deliver the same service repeatedly and reliably. A company gives you help with something, in exchange for your money (and your time). Growth is a function of how many people consider the help worth the price, and profit is a function of how high the price is versus the cost of delivering.

Once upon a time, the lean story starts as an American quality professor, W. Edwards Deming gives a series of influential lectures in devastated post-WWII Japan. At the time, spurred by the US-led reconstruction plan, Japanese industry was shifting fast from craftmanship to mass production. *"Made in Japan"* was synonymous with cheap and shoddy. Deming struck a chord. His talks helped convince Japanese industrial leaders that quality was the key to market domination. He argued that:[2]

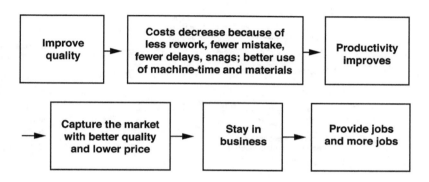

He also suggested that Japanese companies should learn a different way to deliver quality. He proposed they realize higher quality by building it in—teaching each process to control its own quality—as opposed to the Western way of inspecting it out—having a final inspection stage setting aside defective

2    Deming, W. E. (1982) *Out Of The Crisis*, MIT, Center for Advanced Educational Services, Cambridge

products. The key to do so, in his view, was to develop a fuller understanding of the company as a system.[3]

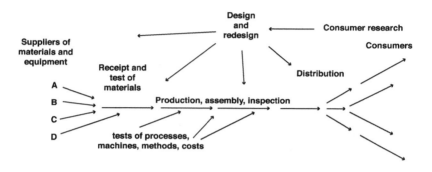

Rather than inspecting the parts at the end of the process, discarding defectives and selecting good ones, he argued for continuous quality testing built into the production and assembly processes.

In the 1950s, one company in particular, Toyota, took up this challenge, and vied successfully for the Deming Prize. "Built in" quality (as opposed to inspected out) resonated with home grown

---

3    The figure is from the same book as the previous.

ideas of "jidoka" (intelligent automation in order to "not accept defectives, not make defectives, not pass on defectives") and the "andon" system of stop-and-call at every defect. Also, in logistics, the radical idea of "just-in-time", the principle to only deliver what is needed, when it's needed, in the quantity needed—was then, on the shop floor, being turned into the most powerful operational learning system ever, by Taiichi Ohno and the kanban system. By following the next process' production instruction (a kanban card) as a close relay of real customer demand (as opposed to relying on centralized scheduling instructions calculated on batches and stock levels) variation in instructions and production were revealed right away, leading to better collaboration between departments across the whole system. Both andon and kanban were test mechanisms: systems to highlight delivery problems in real time, as and when they happened, so that they could be fixed (with "kaizen," small, continuous step by step improvements) and learning could be capitalized by ongoing upgrading of standards.

Toyota leaders also recognized that as the company grew fast it would become fat, slow and inflexible, as is the fate of any company as it ages—and this happens at any size, not just multi-billion corporations. This is the natural consequence of organizing activities for repeatable results: in humans, habits, good or bad, lead to habituation—no longer responding to a specific stimulus, but responding habitually, and then no longer reacting to any stimulus change. While this allows us to build large enterprises, it also makes us rather inefficient as external change is always faster than internal change. The founders and leaders of Toyota understood this early on, and they gave it a name: "Big Company Disease." The four main symptoms of big company diseases are:

- *Defending processes over customers:* as the organization gets set in its way, executives make decisions to make their lives easier, or simply follow their fancies. Meanwhile, customers' tastes evolve, as do their lifestyles. New products are designed as a response of executive pressure, not customer preferences. As a result, the firm finds itself no longer helping as opposed to other alternatives, and loses its customers.

- *Defending silos over teamwork:* specializing work in functional silos is essential to learning to do difficult things. However, functional silos quickly develop their own cultures and start fighting for turf and resources with the other specialties, neglecting the basic fact that the value customers receive is the result of cooperation, collaboration and teamwork across functions.

- *Putting down talented people:* young, talented people tend to challenge the status quo by looking for better, newer way of doing things. They resent absurd policies and feel that competence should be valued over compliance. As a result, they can easily be seen as troublemakers who reject "company standards," and middle-managers will frustrate and castigate them to "protect" the organization from new blood and new ideas.

- *Confusing heritage and legacy technologies:* some technologies are heritage—they've worked effectively in the past, and they still do now. They should be protected from modernism for modernism's sake, lest the company lose exactly what it's prized for. On the other hand, some technologies become antiquated, hold you back, and need abandoning to move on, such as, for example, keeping paperwork on paper, on your hard drive, or in the cloud. Knowing which is which is never easy and needs constant challenging and hard thinking at the workplace to figure it out—or make company-threatening mistakes.

Short of everything, from capital to technology, Toyota leaders were nevertheless determined to be the first to produce affordable cars for everyone, designed by Japanese engineers for Japanese people, with Japanese production staff and suppliers— as opposed to purchasing Western licenses in the early fifties (Nissan from Austin, Isuzu from Rootes, Hino from Renault and Mitsubishi from Willys Jeep) and using Western suppliers. Coming out of a bankruptcy and bank-imposed restructuration, they responded unexpectedly by developing, through trial-and-error, unique *learning systems*, such as:

- *Product-based strategy (*Hoshin Kanri*)* through regular product renewal in every segment to offer cars for everybody and support the "one-time customer, lifelong customer" strategy. How can each customer find a more satisfying product in the product range as their lifestyles evolve, and never need to look elsewhere?

- The *Toyota Product Development* "shusa" *system* (TPDS): Chief Engineer-led product development to integrate the design of cars to create products of reliable quality at an affordable cost while keeping up with trends and technology. How can each new product better carry on what people like about the brand as well as adapt to the spirit of the times?

- The *Toyota Production System* (TPS) to provide a large variety of quality products through a flexible manufacturing system continuously using new ideas to seek the productivity frontier. How could the safest working conditions, highest quality, shortest lead-times and lowest costs be sought by step-by-step improvements from employees' creative ideas?

- *Total Quality Management* (TQM) to draw in staff and back-office operations into developing people for better team-work and more global effectiveness. How can departmental policies change progressively to reflect the improvements made at value-adding work level?

In the late 1980s, an international team of researchers noticed that Toyota had superior performance to its competitors, not in one dimension—but in all! They published their results in the bestseller, *The Machine That Changed The World*,[4] the book that popularized the term "lean." This created a lot of interest in lean thinking, mostly, at the time, focused on improving processes through better organizing the flow of work. Yet, while not incorrect, as Mr. Takehiko Harada, a sensei who has worked directly for Taiichi Ohno, author of *Management Lessons From Taiichi Ohno*[5] explained to us, Western interpretations largely missed what Toyota originally intended with its *Toyota Production System* (from which "lean" was inspired), notably on "training of subordinates" and "total optimization rather than partial optimization."

Lean's core assumption is that *when people better understand what they do and why, they're better at everything they touch.* It follows that understanding is hard work—and that in order to grasp more deeply what one does, one needs to challenge both the

---

4    J. Womack, D. Jones, D. Roos (1990) *The Machine That Changed The World*, Simon & Schuster, New York

5    T. Harada (2015) *Management Lessons From Taiichi Ohno*, McGraw Hill, New York

goals (what outcomes are we seeking?) and the detailed daily work (how are we delivering the outputs that lead to these outcomes?) in order to understand our own responses and change them step by step looking for better ways.[6] Cast in this light lean can be seen as a mindful and proactive systems approach to ongoing learning.

Challenging oneself is never easy. The pressures of just getting the job done are relentless, and we are all always tempted to just get on with things and reduce outcomes (tomorrow's overall situation is better than today's) to a few outputs (let's deliver what they ask even though we can see it doesn't help), and thus keeping everything we do *average*—repeating known mistakes time and time again.

Toyota leaders recognize that the company's success is the result of individual insights, initiative and ingenuity, that management has to orient and support. This is the core insight at

---

6    In theory of knowledge, this is known as "double-loop learning": responding faster to challenges to adapt to new situations (first loop) then studying responses to find more effective, adaptive ones (second loop).

the root of their distinctive way of developing products, each product based on the wisdom and leadership of its Chief Engineer drawing from the skills of engineering teams, or at Toyota's approach to *Total Quality Management* and involving all teams in quality circles or *Toyota's Production System* of making processes visible to reveal problems and get frontline staff to improve things. Each of these unique, enduring initiatives lead to the *continuous development of people*.

The company's main tenet is that *to develop great products, first you have to develop great people*. The hitch is that, for adults learning is mostly about being challenged and questioning their own experience. This is where "sensei" come in. As Akio Toyoda explains: "We say at Toyota that every leader is a teacher developing the next generation of leaders. This is their most important job."

"A real irony is that respect for people requires that people feel the pain of critical feedback. When team members share with us the results of their improvement activities we always say "show us the bad news first. What is it you still have problems with?" If we do not give people accurate feedback based on real behavior they are not growing and we are not respecting them. The job of a leader is not to put them in a position to fail, but to put them in challenging positions where they must work hard to succeed and still see how they could have been better. Our goal is for *every* Toyota team member from the worker on the production floor to our most senior executives to be working to continuously improve themselves. We all need *sensei* who will guide us to the next level of achievement. I personally still have many *sensei* teaching me."[7]

What then, is this mysterious "sensei" role Toyota's President refers to? What is it for? What does it do? How to learn to become a sensei? This short book is by no means a definitive answer to

---

7    J. Liker & G. Convis (2012) *The Toyota Way to Lean Leadership, McGraw-Hill*, New York

that complex question, but maybe a starting point to think about what sensei are and the pivotal place they hold in lean thinking to help executives look up, see the Big Waste in the delivery system (engineering, production, supply chain) from looking at the small waste in everyday work and think differently to improve, themselves first, then their people and, as a result, their departments and the company in full.

1

# WHAT IS A LEAN SENSEI?

As more and more people adopt lean *as a system to continuously develop people*[8] (as opposed to point-by-point process improvement) lean officers are increasingly asked to conduct *gemba walks*

---

8   M. Ballé & T. Richardson (2018) "How Does Asking Questions Create Change", *The Lean Post*, The Lean Enterprise Institute, Boston

with senior managers:[9] this means accompanying top executives to the workplace, whether production, engineering or supply chain to… do what, exactly?

Traditionally, since the word "lean" was coined in the late eighties, one learns lean from participating in gemba walks led by a sensei, and then practicing kaizen through "self-study" projects.

*Sensei* is a made-up word—neither teacher, mentor, coach, consultant nor guru. It first came from martial arts where the sensei is someone knowledgeable, proficient and experienced enough to teach a practice. In the west, our bureaucratic thinking has traditionally separated those roles. The teacher is primarily seen as a classroom teacher that can teach you formal knowledge. The mentor passes on experience. The coach teaches you the practice. The consultant does the analysis and recommendation work for you. The guru is a lifestyle guide.

---

9    *Gemba*, or *Genba*, is a Japanese term that means "the actual place:" where customers use products or services, where products or services are imagined and designed, where they are produced and so forth.

Sensei is not a title you can take for yourself. It is given to you as a sign of respect from the people who want to learn from you because they recognize your mastery, such as it is. This mastery requires a blend of theoretical knowledge, practical skills, and good judgment from experience, as well as a genuine intention to help—even when the lessons can be on the brutal side. Not surprisingly "sensei" involves some amount of grey hair and a sense of having been there before—and so being able to point the way.

The "sensei" role in industry is a Western construct[10]—the Toyota veterans we meet in Japan are often surprised (if not downright amused) at being called sensei and at the whole martial arts terminology (kata, belts, etc.). Toyota is first and foremost a superb technical company, and although in the West we recognized its mastery in production, most of its know-how—the hidden part of the iceberg—is in engineering (and engineering supplier

---

10    It is presented in *Lean Thinking* as meaning "teacher" in Japanese but with the Confucian connotation of "master," in J. Womack & D. Jones (1996) *Lean Thinking*, The Free Press, New York.

development). Toyota has a clear theory of itself both at economic and engineering levels, and production choices are the consequences of these inputs. Although *The Machine That Changed The World* did describe the full strategic thinking of Toyota at the time, most subsequent works and training focused narrowly on operations—largely without understanding the economic and engineering choices underpinning production techniques.

Lean thinking spread beyond Toyota to its contractor network through suppliers joining in the just-in-time supply chain. Toyota veteran executives showed suppliers how to use the pressure of "everything—every delivery" to spot and eliminate waste. They taught supplier CEOs the basics of the TPS and its main tools. Some of these veterans retired from the company and became consultants to Western companies to teach them lean thinking through one-week "kaizen" coaching (as opposed to quality circles and suggestions in Toyota). These sensei would essentially visit operations, point to a specific waste, and support you in improving operations to eliminate it. The misunderstanding was that Western companies thought they were being taught process improvement techniques while the sensei were using process improvement exercises to teach *lean thinking*.

Ask anyone who learned with a sensei back in the late eighties and early nineties what it was like and they'll mostly roll their eyes and say: "we got beaten up, again and again." The sensei, mostly older Japanese gentlemen back then, would take you to the shop floor and:

- *Challenge your discipline:* they'd point places in your processes were clearly things were not happening the way they were supposed to.

- *Give you exercises:* they'd narrow down on one area—without explaining why—and then give you an exercise to do, sketching scantly the technique they wanted you to practice.

- *Give you undivided attention:* they'd seldom validate, agree or encourage, but they would listen patiently to justifications, doubt, issues, impossibilities– and completely ignore what other operational drama was happening at the same time, focusing exclusively on the problem at hand.

- *Push you to the next step:* working with sensei was frustrating on many levels, but mainly because they did not seem interested in the solutions you'd found to the exercises they'd given. They were always demanding more, further, beyond. Their advice was often cryptic and arbitrary, such as "close the warehouse!" "double the frequency of delivery!" "99.5 % good parts is 5000 missed per million!" and so on. They showed the next step, you had to figure out why it was important and how to get there.

One of the authors witnessed the first time a sensei came to talk to the assembled business unit managers of a Toyota supplier. Senior executives had been called from all over the world to meet this elderly gentleman who went straight to an operator station, watched intently for a few minutes, moved a small parts container from a shelf to place it by the operator's hand. Watched some more, moved the container slightly to the side and then nodded to himself looking satisfied. The lecture was over. The group of very senior managers were left completely mystified having to explain to their COO why this very respected Toyota lean master had come all the way from Japan to... do *that*? It took a while to sink in that there was nothing in assembly more important than having components on hand for the operator so that they could work more easily and use two hands at the same time—when the light bulb finally went on, this understanding increased quality and productivity tremendously.

At the time, this was exotic and fun for all of us involved. Learning curves were steep and revealed many conceptual barriers. Sensei learned through a hands-on tradition, each having worked with their own sensei, often having worked directly with Taiichi

Ohno. Different sensei had different approaches, which often seemed at odds one with another. Furthermore, each trainee seemed to draw different conclusions from the sensei sessions: there didn't appear to be a unified body of knowledge. Sensei taught students to think more deeply; but not what to think. At the time, trying to explain what the Toyota system was all about, one sensei did an entire talk with a single slide in the background saying "think deeply!"

This type of teaching came straight out of the birth of lean at Toyota. Nampachi Hayashi, one of the first sensei to teach Western suppliers, recalls his own training with Taiichi Ohno: "I was really afraid of Mr. Ohno when I was young. But I think he was developing thinking people. He never gave us the answer. When he gave us an assignment, he would just stand by and watch us fail, even if he knew the answer."

In the early days of lean, sensei would challenge, sometimes quite harshly, the *status quo* thinking of managers with the aim of opening their eyes to the "real place, real people, real products" reality of the *gemba,* and showing how "to make products, first you have to make people." They would also provide exercises for people to discover this different way of thinking through learning-by-doing. There are many sensei stories going around, sometimes verging on legend or even myth, which begs the question: what do sensei actually do?

# 2

# WHAT DO SENSEI ACTUALLY DO?

If "sensei" is a Western invention, what does the role actually involve in practice? What is the sensei's direct contribution to value? To understand why the sensei's role is different from that of a consultant, coach or mentor we need to understand how minds work—any mind, even the smartest. Our thinking has basically two modes:

- *Delivery:* we are goal-oriented creatures. Western society has reinforced this as much as possible, giving it both its strength in the single-minded pursuit of narrow objectives and its weakness in the tunnel vision that goes with it. Motivated thinking means that every new fact, new idea, new person is seen instrumentally as a way to prove and forward our preset agenda. In the current period, this has been taken to extremes by the Silicon Valley pitch culture where the business case (a complete fantasy pulled out of thin air to convince investors) has to be made real through budgets and action plans to keep investors committed—no matter how reality behaves. Motivated thinking means all thinking is subservient to *a priori* goals and plans.

- *Discovery:* we are also deeply curious creatures, open to exploration and experimentation as long as it's fun and not too risky. We also have a strong aesthetic sense to appreciate things because they are beautiful, new, right, smart, true, cool, exciting, regardless of results. As people get older, the childish sense of curiosity gives progressively way to a sense of awe and wisdom, but we clearly have greater appreciation for things than what they're meant for and what they're worth. The discovery mode is one of asking oneself how new facts and new people can completely change how we understood a situation and look for doors where we thought were brick walls.

Leading any business, one runs into a deep contradiction. On the one hand, everything is structured to reach targets through carrying out plans. Organizations are built for delivery. Yet, new problems require new ideas. Solutions to existing problems often come from thinking outside the box, from seeing what others don't see. Try figure out which number the car is parked on:

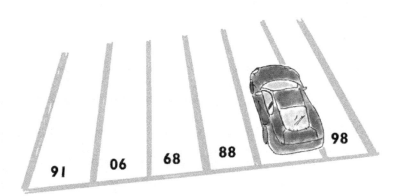

Now turn the sheet around:

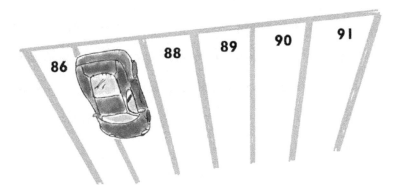

For example, traditionally, any activity is structured so that managers decide who does what when, and a specialist staff department checks quality (this is the way it works from factory shop floor to software development). After Deming's lectures in Japan, Kaoru Ishikawa and Taiichi Ohno turned this on its head and Japanese companies learned to schedule work through a pull system that transmits customer demand mechanically through kanban, and is piloted by a staff *Production Control and Logistics* office. Quality control and training became the central responsibility of line managers. With this method, frontline managers could no longer say "drop this and do that," and not worry about quality. They must plan resources so as not to interrupt the smooth flow of kanban cards and then jump in at each quality alert to make sure they deliver only good work to the next step, and train and train and train: a radical rethink of delivery.

Difficult problems require real thinking: manipulating mental objects until we see them differently, not simply repeating what we already know. As inventor after inventor shows, while people are trying to optimize what is on the table, the next generation of success will come from exploiting an idea *off* the table. This contradiction basically explains why there are still so many management articles written (one would have thought we'd covered the topic by now). Half the papers are about how to better optimize your delivery, and the other half is about chastising leaders for not practicing discovery and completely missing game-changers.

The sensei role is a countermeasure to the overwhelming mental model of motivated thinking with a pressure on delivery, the cherry-picking of facts and actions to justify existing goals and plans—and contribute some space to think for discovery. This is at complete odds with what a consultant does, which is optimize the organization for better collective delivery, or what a coach does, which is to help individuals improve their personal delivery. The sensei's contribution to value is in keeping the spirit of discovery strong through three main ways:

- *Thoughtfulness:* studying the current delivery processes to discover whether things work as planned. Studying quality and on-time delivery, right *now*, to see and hear what reality feeds back and discover how front-line staff cope everyday with systems misaligned with customers' needs and wishes.

- *Awareness:* opening minds to looking elsewhere, looking at the problem differently, challenging what seems obvious but is in fact a deployment of the established goals and plans, and making leaders aware that markets are changing and that the current way of doing things is no longer the best fit.

- *Inventiveness:* pushing people to find different answers to existing problems and, whilst not providing answers, relentlessly asking for concrete next step: What will you try next? What do you think is the problem? How would you go about it? Where would you start from, concretely? How will you know if it works or not?

A president of Toyota's South African operation tells of his sensei visiting the plant when he was plant manager, and pointing to paper being blown in the wind across the aisles of the factory shop floor. "This is Africa, sensei," the plant manager explained. "It's the wind…" After thinking it through for a moment, the sensei replied "wind don't make paper." In this anecdote the sensei is working on both *awareness*—be aware of the production conditions in the plant with loose paper flying around—and *thoughtfulness*—your answer doesn't make logical sense: wind does not produce paper.

Contrarily to consulting, training or coaching, the sensei doesn't have to know the answers (why would she? this is a discovery exercise) but she does have to have a good idea of where to look. In practice, the sensei will:

1. *Take you to the gemba:* take the leader to the real place where customers use the service and where frontline staff do the

work in order to observe firsthand what is really happening as opposed to what it says on the PowerPoint slides and what we *believe* is happening. The sensei's first role is to maintain the dialogue with reality by looking at specific, detailed cases of failure to deliver, such as customer complaints, rework and late deliveries. Go and see is not simply about observing, but about grappling with concrete problems to grasp what constraints apply and how solid they really are—in order to understand the problem more deeply.

2. *Discuss what the real challenges are:* business conversations are implicitly oriented towards goals (here's what we want to achieve) and plans (here's what we need to do). The sensei's role is to question the implicit assumptions in these instructions by trying to get people to agree on the problem before arguing about solutions. This is mostly an exercise in logic: clarifying the causality of both what the goals really

are—often contradictory and unclear—and how the plans can get you there—often a dotted line built on beliefs, faith and wishful thinking rather than logic. Rather than say "I disagree," a sensei will say, "I really don't understand how doing this will deliver what you intend." The sensei's job is to clarify the main challenges that the company needs to face to thrive, rather than help implement ready-to-use solutions.

3. *Prescribe exercises:* real learning is not an "aha!" moment of clear understanding with a life-changing before and after. Real learning emerges from familiarizing oneself with a new thought or practice until it becomes natural. To help people explore what is off the table, the sensei will give concrete exercises, such as "5S" or "measure lead-time" or "stop at the next doubt on quality and have a look." These practical exercises are described extensively in the *Toyota Production System* and are meant to get leaders and their

teams to learn by doing through discovering a difficult issue in concrete, detailed cases. TPS tools are not instrumental tools for random improvements but specific exercises to analyze and solve recurring problems, linked to key business challenges. SMED is not about reducing tool changes, it's about learning to run shorter batches, something no one is at ease with in the way our organizations are designed for delivery at the lowest unit cost. The exercises don't have a predetermined answer—again, this is discovery, not delivery—but the people themselves will discover their answers through carrying out the exercise repeatedly.

4. *Teach PDCA:* While exercises are there to develop awareness, thoughtfulness, depth of thinking, is just as important. Thinking deeply means going beyond the fast reaction of memory and engaging the slow thinking processes of considering ideas against what we see and know and kicking

them around. It's hard—both personally and socially. To really understand something, we have to try to change it—the commitment to change is what gets us looking seriously at an idea, and examining how reality reacts. In its internal manual to On-The-Job development, Toyota describes itself as a sum of PDCA cycles leading to "long-term prosperity and growth as an organization."[11]

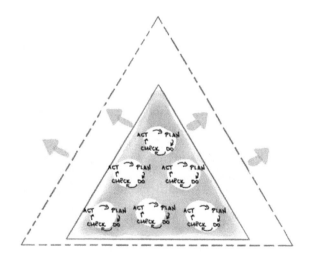

---

11    *On The Job Development*, (2007) Toyota Institute, Toyota Motor Corporation

The main guideline to think deeply is Deming's Plan-Do-Check-Act (PDCA) cycle: clarify a change you *plan* to test and why, *do* it in a limited way, on a small scale to see what happens if you carry it out, *check* the impact, quantifiably if you can or looking very carefully if you can't, and *act* upon it, decide whether you want to adopt the change, adjust it or abandon it. Because motivated thinking is dominant, most people do plan/do, plan/do, plan/do and never check/act. The sensei is there to make sure the PDCA cycle is carried out in full so that people *actually think* and not stay satisfied with their quick responses.

Awareness
- What we get
- What we don't get
- What we get wrong?
- What is critically important right now (are we missing it?)

DISCOVERY

Built-In Quality, Dialogue with reality

Find, Face, Frame, Form

DELIVERY

Thoughtfulness
- Going deeper into concrete problems to understand the source causes...
- asking "why?" one more time

5. *Push you on to the next step:* Sensei never seem satisfied with what you've done and are always asking: What next? Hajime Ohba, a long-time Toyota sensei with suppliers in North America, explains that "True North" thinking always concerns what we need to do, not what we can do. His approach is typical of what we've seen other sensei do: Think deeply about what you see on the gemba and try your idea immediately; Do small and gradual experiments to relate the method to people's work. Always ask the question "What's next?" Don't dwell on how much better we are but how much farther we have to go. This sums up an approach where thinking can only be done by doing, and where learning occurs when you go beyond the first, or even second attempt to explore the really new and unfamiliar. It's not that the sensei is "never satisfied" as many people feel it, but that the sensei is looking beyond the horizon of what is currently known, for that new practical

idea that will break the back of one constraint and open a new space for improvement.

The sensei's direct contribution to value lies in showing the relationship between delivery and discovery and making sure the balance stays… balanced.

In one plant, the business unit manager was very worried about a new cell that had recently been delivered by engineering—he couldn't see how his cost targets could be achieved with the process he'd been given. He explained that the cell's costs were killing him, and the sensei nodded and asked him about his quality level. "No problem," answered the plant manager, who was present. "Our quality is very good." "Yes, but what is it?" insisted the sensei. "Oh, we are below the single digit bad parts per million," explained the plant manager—which is indeed incredibly good. "So, you have very few bad parts?" puzzled the sensei. "Yes, we have very few bad parts," rejoined the plant

manager exasperated, "however, the cost structure of the cell—"
"they must then be very interesting," interrupted the sensei,
"please show me the latest bad part." Ultimately, it turned out
that solving the remaining quality problems on the cell led to a
deeper understanding of the technologies, and then modifications
that brought the cost of use down considerably—solving the
original cost concern.

Why did the sensei insist on quality rather than look into the
cost problem right away? Because the sensei follows a different
theory. The business unit manager is looking at this budget and
identifying problems line by line:

- Cost of non-quality: okay since we have very few defects

- Cost of operation: bad since we're too costly overall

As any manager would, he focuses on the lines that are not
okay, trying to find a mitigation plan that will fix his delivery

so he can move on to a different issue. The sensei, on the other hand, has no particular pressure to deliver—not his immediate problem—but intends to teach the manager how to better deliver through a process of discovery, which requires understanding the problem more fully. Rather than solving the problem line by line, he is guided by another thought: good results come from good processes (in this context, understand "process" as *a method to do something repeatably*):

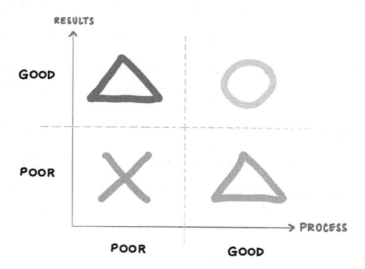

We can joke that it's better to be lucky than good, any day, but it's hard to be lucky every day. Lucky is when you have good results without quite understanding why. On the other hand, sticking to a known method and delivering poor results is plain stupid (not that this stops anyone).

The sensei *knows* that quality problems are caused by gaps in understanding in the physical process used to make the parts. The sensei also knows that these gaps in understanding will be compensated in everyday life by shop-floor management through extra resources. On the other hand, the sensei has no idea what these problems are or how the people compensate (and hide) them locally.

Rather than follow the business unit manager's *delivery* reasoning of quality performance➔quality action and cost performance➔cost action, the sensei starts an investigation of the problem by thinking quality➔gap in process understanding. By orienting the local team towards concrete quality issues to better understand the delivery process in details, the sensei has a solid hope that they will discover the levers to reduce costs (essentially, taking out compensating actions) by learning what parameters to control more tightly.

In this specific case, the problem turned out to be a supplier quality issue which had not been identified and which caused setbacks all over the place. The sensei had no way of knowing that, but had the experience to know where to look and the theory to start them looking—as well as the credibility to get them to look at something they felt would not solve their problem in the short term.

Sensei-ing differs from other sorts of expert contribution because sensei are not supposed to know the answers. As with scientific advisors, they are, however, supposed to have a very good understanding of the questions. Lean officers and consultants are expected to master the lean tools and to be able to facilitate groups in order to achieve performance improvement through process improvements. Sensei, however, are expected to develop people in order to grow the business as a whole—quite a different challenge. What does one need to know to go beyond consulting or coaching and start sensei-ing?

# 3

# WHAT DO SENSEI KNOW?

Today lean ideas have spread across the business world. This group of authors has seen countless examples of companies that have thrived with lean, at a time where the financial/bureaucratic approach of mainstream management is increasingly recognized as wasteful both of people and resources. Slowly but surely, more companies want to implement lean "the right way," their leadership intent on *gemba walks* and *kaizen* (as opposed to corporate programs seeking "savings" from process mapping, improvement projects and daily rituals). Unfortunately, most of the old-time sensei have retired for good, presenting the thorny problem of increased demand for sensei to conduct gemba walks, but no clear idea on where to find them or how to develop new sensei.

By now, there are many lean officers trained in lean concepts and experienced in leading kaizen improvement workshops, but it seems that the leap to sensei is a hard one: one has to convince senior managers to be coached on the shop floor, to convince frontline managers to conduct their own self-study activities and to convince employees that participating in improvement is in their best interest. What is the big difference between lean officers and sensei?

- Lean officers teach lean techniques to operators and front-line leaders to eliminate waste in processes.

- Sensei investigate waste and use problem-solving to teach executives to better understand their customers, their products or services, their delivery processes and how to become more competitive.

Although sensei are not expected to know the answers to the questions they ask (this is the work of the leaders who need to discover their own answers), sensei nevertheless need to know how to ask the right questions. This means that sensei constantly cultivate their awareness of the current state of the business, its products and its delivery processes.

The sensei role progressively came into being as Western executives tried to make sense of what Toyota veterans were teaching. They discovered that these Toyota grey-hairs had:

1. Inside-out knowledge of the automotive industry, having made their entire careers in it and, for some of them,

having seen it take off from scratch in the sixties and seventies in Japan.

2. In-depth understanding of automobiles as a product, many of the them having been involved with the design or start of production of the early mass-manufactured Toyota cars.

3. Deep personal experience of the evolution of production systems, from traditional Fordism to Toyotism, having had a direct hand in developing the hodgepodge mix of improvement exercises that became the TPS.

4. A tradition of teaching through learning-by-doing by setting oneself tough-to-impossible challenges and striving to resolve them astutely, having been taught themselves in that fashion.

If you add translation issues, cultural differences in teaching mode, a generally authoritarian style specific to Toyota managers (by all means, not all Toyota veterans are as peremptory as the first shop floor guys), and so on, no wonder Western engineers struggled with what to make of these early teachers and came up with a mythical image of "sensei" as seen in popular culture, somewhere between Mr. Miyagi in *The Karate Kid* and Master Splinter in *Teenage Mutant Ninja Turtles*.

The fact remains that for successful sensei-ing, a sensei has to develop his or her exploration and knowledge of what the right questions are by studying:

1. *The business in its industry:* business environments change faster than most companies. Organizations are sticky (actually designed to be so). For instance, contrarily to the image it tries to give, Toyota is a very aggressive competitor and has led with fast product development and a diverse lineup, in the 1960s, through greater flexibility to attack the Japanese market. Then, quality and standard options to attack the American market in the 1980s. Then green

with hybrid in the 1990s and now is fighting back on the connectivity revolution started by Tesla. In any industry the frontline changes, such as moving from mainframes to micro-computers, to PC operating systems, to browser led-platforms, to digitalizing and cloud in the IT sector. Most companies are stuck fighting the previous war, such as companies trying to digitalize their old ways of working, and the sensei has to be able to ask the right questions to orient on frontlines to win the current war.

2. *Product evolution:* industry pressures are reflected in product design. Cars, for instance, first had to be easy to maintain yourself (Ford Model T), then had to be fashionable, then safe, then robust, then energy efficient, then connected and so on. This evolution is reflected in engineering designs and choices, and all main components have a learning curve (as is displayed in the Toyota Memorial museum). A sensei

need not be expert at every aspect of design of the product, clearly, but needs to be aware of the evolutionary pressures on the product and kind of solution picked by the company's engineering—as opposed to what others have done. Or at the very, very least, be interested in product evolution.

3. *Production system history:* the delivery processes adapt not only to product or service evolution, but also other pressures such as relentless demands for optimization from corporate or regulatory changes. Here again, the sensei needs to be aware of the history of these changes to understand why processes are the way they are. Today's delivery processes are most likely the results of layer after layer of control systems—from managerial to IT—which explains a large part of their low performance and rigidity. However, to ask the right question, the sensei needs to have some sense of how this happened and the pressures that remain on the production system.

4. *Basic understanding of how people's minds work*: since the sensei's job is to get people to think, and then to think more deeply, a basic understanding of thinking is useful, such as distinguishing the (fast) reaction of memory from the (slow) process of frame-control and looking at whether ideas are more or less likely. Thinking processes are mostly like kids' slides—once on the chute, straight to the forgone conclusion. People think by formulating constraints, testing them according to the necessities of the situation, and drawing new fledgling conclusions they then have to sell to their peers. Minds are built so that what is easier to process feels more credible, and nothing is easier to process than what we see (zero effort, it goes straight to the brain). A good grasp of basic thinking processes and common biases goes a long way in the sensei-ing job.

In one of the legendary sensei stories, a Toyota sensei was observing a robot painting parts at a supplier. Then he left the plant, went back in town and bought a bathroom blow dryer. Hairdryer in hand, he showed the assembled engineers how to dry painted parts and what kind of movement the robot had trouble following. Mr. Oba had proved to incredulous engineers that their $280,000 investment was undermining quality and pushing up costs.[12] The anecdote reflects the deep technical knowledge Toyota sensei often have within their own area of operation— knowledge which would be almost impossible to replicate as one explores other domains, but that should remain a guiding star. Understanding frameworks is not enough—one has to challenge oneself to always try to discover "blow dryer" level knowledge in both engineering and operations.

The first discovery topic in lean thinking is *value*, looking for

---

12    N. Shirouzu (2001) "How does Toyota Maintain Quality: Mr. Oba's Hair Dryer Offers A Clue," *The Wall Street Journal*, March 15

how products and services help customers solve their problems within their (evolving) lifestyles. Then we move on to *value analysis* by solving delivery problems in the existing production processes, which helps us understand the deeper engineering problems that have to be resolved through *value engineering*, improving designs at the concept phase to better fit products and services to what customers like. This gets us to face our deeper competency deficiencies and address them through concrete step by step learning curves.

One of the main differences between the sensei approach and traditional consulting is that sensei look outward to understand issues in broader terms, whilst consultants look inward to adopt generic tools that can be packaged and are supposed to work in every circumstance. The sensei starts with "why?", the consultant starts with "how." To learn to grow as a sensei one has to accept that Toyota didn't just do one thing repetitively, but in the critical years of the 1960s, Eiji Toyoda supported the encouragement of several learning systems: a better economic theory, with "*hoshin kanri*," starting from product planning all the way to policy deployment; a better product theory, with the *Product Development System* of Chief Engineers; a better production theory, with the *Toyota Production System;* a better management theory with *Total Quality Management.*

We six authors have all started by learning the consultant's way: take one tool and apply it in all cases. Generally, this tool is some form of process mapping. Michael was putting brown paper in rooms back in the previous century and mapping the process in detail with post-it notes, then estimating a throughput time (how long does it take from start to finish) and a process efficiency (% of value-added task to total time) and looking for ways to improve the process (embarrassingly, he even wrote a book about it[13]). The rest of us learned the "lean" method of *Value Stream Mapping*, which is in fact very similar, with some

---

13    M. Ballé, (1995) The Business Process Re-engineering Action Kit, Kogan Page, London

lean aspects. This is as good starting point as any, since you've got to map the process path in any case, but then the consultant and the sensei part ways. The consultant will apply the tool with greater and greater rigor and in all cases, while the sensei will set upon the lifelong learning path of understanding the wider view.

A process is mostly a sequence of dependent steps driven by:

**Instructions → Production → Stock or backlog**

People aren't stupid—most processes are sound. But then all sorts of things in the environment affect the process and add variation to the mix:

**Instructions variations → Production variations → Stock fluctuation**

All of these dynamics feed back into each other and create an incomprehensible, inefficient mess. Without a deeper insight into the whole systems, most direct actions reflect the pillow

WHAT DO SENSEI KNOW?

syndrome: squeeze here, it bulges there. The Sensei's skill lies in understanding the source of variation in both environment and production conditions—more specifically, how people interpret outside unexpected events and turn them into day-to-day decisions, often to unexpected effect. Where the consultant looks inward to straighten out one cause, the sensei looks outward to understand the conditions explaining the cause.

Yes, this might seem like a lot to know, but on the other hand, the sensei path is first a learner's path: to be a teacher, first you need to be a learner. Take a concrete example of one operation several of us know well. Imagine a plant for refurbishing used cars to resale (think of an industrial-sized garage). This plant ensures no mechanical problems at all (the company will sell you a car that runs reliably), will fix fixable body issues and display clearly on photos the remaining problems (so you know what you're buying). This plant was first designed on lean principles by a consultant using Value Stream Mapping. The plant has achieved to produce 700 cars a month.

Because the company is growing, the plan is to build a second site to double monthly capacity, which requires an investment of about 10 million dollars, plus operating expenses of about 500,000 dollars a year.

When the sensei walks into the plant, he asks: "what was your best production day, ever?" What he has in mind is a theory of productivity:

1. *Asset productivity*: how do we fully utilize existing capacity?

2. *People productivity*: how does the way we work impact asset utilization?

3. *Materials productivity*: how do the components and materials we use impact how we work (and what rework and rescheduling we do) and so asset productivity?

From the plant manager's answer, the sensei suggests there is no need to build a second site—the problem is improving production with the current assets. True potential means taking the best performance figures, due to exceptional circumstances, and applying it to every day work. This scopes the work to be done: make the unpredictable predictable, and the exceptional repeatable.

The plant manager of course rebels and argues this is impossible, but the owner is interested and asks how it could be possible. The sensei then acknowledges not knowing, but the place to start is TPS—implementing the basics of just-in-time (a pull system) and jidoka (an andon system to identify problems on the spot)—and then solving problems.

After just a few months, the plant has doubled its production on the best days, mostly due to better understanding the supply of difficult parts and planning the work accordingly, and inventory has drastically diminished. The plant manager discovered that production instructions were dependent on expectations of what parts would be available, as opposed to plan for demand and make sure the needed parts would be sourced. This created a huge backlog of work on cars that were parked all over the plant waiting for the right parts: unnecessary inventory. The performance improvement is spectacular, however it is also very unstable and on average, production has increased significantly, but not enough to compensate for a second site.

At which stage the sensei turns to TQM tools: "Obeya" room management with A3 plans and A3 problem solving, Daily Visual Management on the shop floor with 4M problem solving (Manpower, Machine, Material, Method issues) with the aim of supporting the TPS work in improving back-office procedures. Progressively this increases production every day, from better planning (less "*mura*," instability of work demand) and management of people and suppliers (less "*muri*," overburden and asking people to do unreasonable things) and so being closer to target every day (less "*muda*," wasted work in daily activities).

mura → muri → muda
unlevelness    overburden    waste

As a result, two years later, production has increased from 700 cars a month to 1200 cars a month, at a total investment cost of $100K. The owner estimates that he better serves real customer demand whilst having saved $13M in cash from avoiding the investment and running cost of the planned second plant, with a positive impact on EBITDA of $500K a year. Cars used to need 7 to 10 days to be processed; now 70% of the volume is turned around in less than 3 days and lead-time is a third of what it used to be. This, is *lean*.

The next step, is to turn to the *Product Development System* to understand how the much faster turnaround of cars in the plant from a drastically reduced lead-time (as a result of TPS and TQM activities) can become a competitive advantage by offering radically quicker delivery to customers or other benefits.

The sensei-ing sequence we see here is:

Scoping the system-level gains with *Hoshin Kanri* ➜ Visualizing processes on the gemba, to reveal problems, to start solving them immediately with the *Toyota Production System* ➜ Avoiding backsliding and stabilizing successful experiments by changing management procedures with *Total Quality Management* ➜ looking to improve customer offering with the *Product Development System.*

**Hoshin Kanri:**
better understand the business problem and scope the true potential, and involving the whole organization in catchball plans

**Toyota Production System:**
get people started by visualizing processes, revealing problems, and hands on try-and-see, try-and-see

**Product Development System:**
Guaranteeing future results by integrating the learning into the next generation of products and processes

**Total Quality Management:**
avoid backsliding by involving back-office work in creating better management procedures through systematizing PDCA

The sensei doesn't have to know everything about these four learning systems, and certainly doesn't have to know much about the production processes itself to start with. To be successful however, the sensei has to exert herself or himself to learn more daily—both about the lean learning systems and the specifics of the gemba production methods and management thinking. In this, would-be sensei need to adopt the fundamental perspective of lean thinking:

- There are correct answers but they remain hidden—we don't know them so we have to look for them;

- There are however known mistakes that we can avoid (regardless of how intent many managers are of doing them again, and again);

- And continue to look for workable answers by gemba learning and problem-solving to learn what we can from local counter-measures to hands on exercises;

- We have known methods to start the investigation. These methods are a starting point, not an end point.

The challenge is not knowing beforehand, but knowing where to seek when one does not: where do we start the learning process, what is the direction for learning, what are the known, classic pitfalls to avoid.

To become a sensei, one need not know everything about everything about the business. One needs, however to be genuinely interested in the context that produced the existing delivery system and in the current challenges. Still, sensei are not general business advisors, and their role is tightly linked to lean thinking. Knowing the lean tools and principles that originate in Toyota is clearly important, but so is understanding more deeply what these tools and principles do for the business. When all is said and done, a sensei as a learner will always return to studying the basics of TPS time and time again. What is so critical about TPS?

# 4

# WHAT IS THE TPS ACTUALLY FOR?

To the sensei, out of these many learning systems that Toyota has developed, the *Toyota Production System* remains essential: the foundational practice. The TPS sets the conditions for *kaizen*, for taking that next step, facing that challenge, attacking what needs to be done beyond what we know how to do, and doing this on the gemba, with the teams themselves by looking deeply into work and trying ideas on the spot. Yes, TQM is essential to make sure improvements don't backslide by involving managers in improving their own procedures in order to standardize kaizen successes. Yes, the TPDS is key to a product-driven strategy and to developing products people buy by developing engineers' thinking and knowledge. And, yes, Hoshin Kanri is crucial to have all leaders in the company come together to respond to challenges, from the front lines to the executive boardroom. But TPS is where the spirit of improvement lies.

Lean is not a production system, it's an education system. The "TPS" name itself is unfortunate and misleading as it suggests this is a collection of production practices to copy. Indeed, some Toyota veterans have told us they prefer to call it the *Thinking People System*.[14] The trouble is that, many people think they can replace their current practices with the "best"

---

14   M. Ballé, G. Beauvallet, A. Smalley, D. Sobek (2006) "The Thinking Production System," *Reflections*, 7:2

practices of the TPS. They fail to understand that the TPS evolved as the sum of responses Toyota discovered as it faced specific obstacles. Rather than a system of practices, Toyota engineers came up with a system of learning: a way to discover problems and resolve them. The aim is not to replace one's own production system by Toyota's (which doesn't make much sense when you think it through), but to use the TPS to improve your own productions system by teaching better thinking—everyone, everywhere, every day.

In this context, the sensei is there to help leaders first see the existing production system as it is: what are the instructions? how are they realized in practice? with what outcomes? how does what we see differ from what we thought we would see?

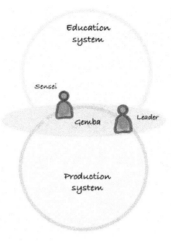

The starting point to do so is to look for waste and explore the causes of waste, by changing the way things are currently done and looking hard at what happens. In practice, by challenging everyone for local initiatives. This stage is a bit tricky because, as we saw in the preceding chapter, we're seeking a "helicopter" vision (from the big picture to the narrowest detail) of looking for both:

- *Occurrence* problems: detailed diversion from how things are supposed to happen to understand what concrete obstacles stop the existing process from being perfectly repeatable.

- *Target* problems: large issues that constrain the existing process in achieving its overall growth objectives, such as stopping recruitment to fit with the budget, emptying inventories at financial year end, planning production according to batches and all aspects of created demand; not following real customer demand but planning on internal constraints.

Having solved the concrete problems emerging from visualizing processes more clearly, we then need to share the changes adopted with the rest of the organization so that they can adapt their interfaces and systems as well, and think deeply about what this means for the entire company, looking for potential innovations—and promoting innovators.

As an education system, the TPS is a set of production practices aimed at revealing problems so that people can react quickly to avoid defects or missed shipments, and then reflect more deeply on the causes and conditions of these occurrences:

See the existing production system as it is: what are the instructions? how are they realized in practice? with what outcomes? how does what we see differ from what we thought we would see?

Visualize processes with customer satisfaction, just-in-time, jidoka, heijunka, standardized work, 5S and TPM techniques to support problem solving and kaizen in order to reveal problems and get everyone involved in thinking about what they do

Look for waste and explore the causes of waste by changing the way things are currently done and looking hard at what happens, by challenging everyone for local initiatives.

Share the changes adopted with the rest of the organization so that they can adapt their interfaces and systems as well, and thinking deeply about what this means for the entire company, looking for potential innovations—and promoting innovators.

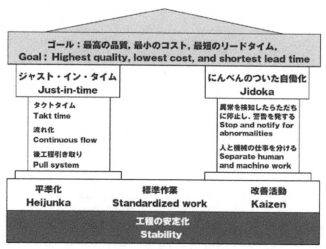

トヨタ生産方式の基本のイメージ：TPSハウス
Basic Image of the Toyota Production System: the TPS House

Source: Kaizen Express

*Visual management* is the sensei's own area of direct expertise and they will typically point to flaws in the visual conditions of work to always push for greater visualization of the work cells themselves. But they can use visual management to convey larger points as well. For example, one sensei asked the management team of a Toyota forklift plant to draw an A0 map of the process, drawing a circle for every crate of component inventory. At the end of each visit, he'd cross out circles, visualizing how the plant should learn to work with less and less on hand inventories.

*100% right first time with zero inventory* is an educational device to push the company to explore what it does in detail and progressively clarify the grey areas until quality is delivered repeatedly at low cost. The TPS is a set of principles and exercises (the tools) that support the sensei in doing the real job of discussing challenges and deepening the thinking through hands-on learning. Certainly, the more at ease the sensei is with the lean tools, the easier the job. But mastery of the lean tools is not the only tricky problem sensei need to face.

Experienced sensei tell you there is no knowing the TPS, there is only learning the TPS. The more you practice it, the more you see it as a system and understand how the various principles interact. But to understand the TPS more deeply, you also need to be curious about the other learning systems and how they relate to the TPS. Again, the aim here is not total mastery of everything, but a curiosity and seeking to know more.

For instance, a large piece of the puzzle of Toyota's success is its Total Quality Management system: starting from basic Statistical Process Control and a creative idea suggestion system in the 1950s, it expanded the idea of total participation to Quality Circles for frontline teams, A3s for managers and a variety of initiatives promoting quality and teamwork such as *"Mizenboushi"* (prevention) or *"Jikotei Kantetsu"* (building quality into each process), all aiming to make quality personal and craft it into the company's DNA as its lifeline.

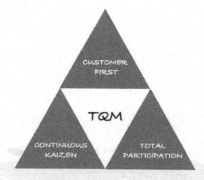

Much less is known of its *Product Development System*, as the company considers it a competitive secret, but from what is communicated to close suppliers, a rough idea can be sketched out:[15]

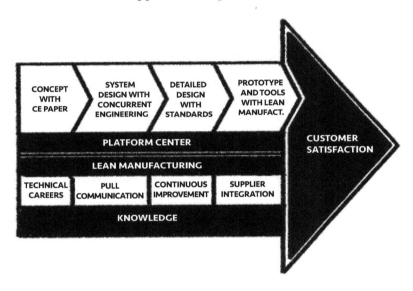

The main problem a Chief Engineer faces, as we hear time and time again in Toyota City, is how to make the most daring car to best please customers, whilst understanding that customers' first choice preferences are robustness (no hassles, high resale

---

15    Ballé, F., Ballé, M. (2005) "Lean Development", *Business Strategy*, LBS

value) and price. People want a fun, attractive car, that is fun and safe to drive, that never breaks and that they can afford. Toyota's way to balance these trade-offs is to ask one person, the Chief Engineer, to navigate a difficult path between:

- *Bold new features:* what new things will be added?

- *Sustaining company standards* on quality, flexibility (the car has to fit with other cars on the line) and cost: what will we keep without touching it?

Indeed, one of the hidden strengths of Toyota is its mix of planning know-how. Product planning is a mesh between:

- *A takt time of new models for each car/segment:* The corolla, for instance, was introduced in 1966 and is now in its twelfth generation, with a new model presented every four years. Each new model follows the same general concept, for instance in the corolla's case it's "an affordable family car with a few luxury features" as it has been from the start. Each new model must achieve a grade of 80% on a list of performances, and then a "plus alpha"—strive for 90% on a few key aspects.

- *A mix of products offered by region*: variety offered in each region is planned, so that the mix for sale corresponds to the 20% of models covering 80% of the demand in that region: what is for sale locally is a small subset of all available products, types and options.

- *A mix of products per plant*: Toyota aims to have production closest to its markets, but also juggles with fast product renewal and flexibility. "Mother" plants in Japan can handle as many as 8 different models on the same production line. "Daughter" plants in the rest of the world learn flexibility slowly, as the first emphasis is on quality. As with the regional sales mix, the volume attributed to less flexible plants is the minimum that is expected to sell, and if sales go beyond capacity, the extra demand is taken up by the flexible plants in Japan where the law of large numbers balances peaks and troughs.

- *Product complexity reduction*: this multiple-dimensions equation can easily get out of hand, so the company is always seeking to reduce complexity wherever it can, by finding opportunities to use common design, components and suppliers across car models—as a result, for instance, it often considers to make high-volume options standard (air conditioning) and to eliminate low demand options (ashtrays).

The upshot of this rigorous product planning is that a new model is slated to be developed with scope, volume and cost targets—and then handed over to a Chief Engineer, who, like a fashion designer, will be responsible for all the product choices all the way to introducing the car on the market, although he has no formal authority over any of the functional departments. The

TPDS takes over from product planning at the "concept paper" phase when the Chief Engineer explains his plan to make the car a success in response of the challenge offered by product planning.

Once again, no would-be sensei needs to know the details of all of this, but it is important to realize that Toyota's old-time sensei worked in an environment where these different elements were a given, which oriented much of the way they interpreted the TPS. As a teacher/learner, we don't have to know, but that shouldn't stop us from continuously seeking and looking up beyond the borders of TPS to the other ingredients in Toyota's unique lean approach.

Profitability at company level is precisely the topic that interests CEOs and other senior executives. Yes, they can see that precision in operations is one key to their effectiveness, but without the link to wider strategy, they often fail to appreciate the impact of lean thinking on their business as a whole. Seeing the big picture means relating higher customer satisfaction (which starts with better product planning), through better products (which means developing value—fit-to-use features at a reasonable price), from improved production processes (TPS and TQM) and tighter links to suppliers and other technology partners.

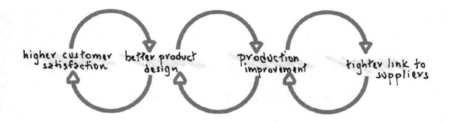

higher customer satisfaction    better product design    production improvement    tighter link to suppliers

Sensei work at CEO or COO level and their aim is not to solve one problem and improve one process, but to show how to create the conditions for systematic problem solving and kaizen in order to orient the company towards greater competitiveness. Knowing the lean concepts and techniques forms a necessary basis, absolutely, but the next step requires:

1. *Recognizing teachable problems:* detailed operational problems with a strategic impact.

2. *Working with senior executives:* understanding C-level language and worldview.

3. *Handling observation and discussion at the workplace:* confronting operators with senior people in the company on their own workplace is socially awkward and needs to be managed.

4. *Choosing "next step" developmental problems:* helping executives and managers to enrich their understanding by solving meaningful problems that are neither too removed from their context, nor too mundane.

5. *Developing visual management:* spreading the techniques necessary to make work visually intuitive and reveal problems to be solved autonomously during day-to-day work.

Committing to learning the TPS inside out is not an end point for a sensei—it's a starting point. No one fully understands the entire subtlety of the TPS because it's a system and all its elements interact. For instance, increasing just-in-time tension makes no sense without jidoka to spot problems as they appear, which makes no sense without people who are confident in their standards (currently known way of doing things) and keen to kaizen (look for a better way)—and none of this can happen without a degree of basic stability, which involves a culture of 4M problem solving: stable manpower, stable equipment, stable components and materials, stable methods and so on.

The TPS is a starting point because its rigorous application is where the energy to look for improvement surges from. Mr. Oba is quoted as comparing the way Western managers use lean techniques to improve productivity or slash inventory to "creating a Buddha image and forgetting to inject soul into it."[16] The soul of the TPS is the kaizen spirit: no process is ever perfect, so we always need to look for a better way and rely on people's talent and passion to try something else.

As Joe Lee, Toyota's Taiwan sensei reminded us, "sensei needs to keep a beginner's mind," and always remember that, like the blind men facing an elephant, the parts—the trunk, tusks, ear, belly legs or tail—don't make the whole. Our aim is therefore to continuously study TPS and see where it leads into the other education systems like Hoshin Kanri, TQM or TPDS. TPS is the bedrock of the sensei's skill, but not the be-all and end-all if the sensei truly intends to develop the thinking and understanding of the people he or she works with, on the gemba. To be a good teacher, first be a good learner.

---

16    N. Shirouzu & S. Moffett (2004) "As Toyota Closes In on GM, Quality Concerns Also Grow," *The Wall Street Journal*, August 4, 2004

5

# WHAT IS A SUCCESSFUL GEMBA WALK?

Sensei work mainly through "gemba walks"—taking senior leaders to the workplace and discussing the link between corporate strategy and detailed operations *in situ*. How can the mere fact of executive presence at the workplace improve the company's competitiveness? This is a valid question because… it depends.

As we've learned with the failure of "management by walking around", executive presence is a double-edged sword: it can help, or it can hinder. Success hinges on maintaining a balance between delivery and discovery. Management is obsessed with delivery, rightly so, the sensei's role is to focus on discovery. This is what makes successful gemba walks both incredibly enriching and very fraught. Managers expect immediate solutions to their delivery problems. Sensei know the solution won't be found in the current way the problem is framed, so they keep pushing exploration beyond what is obviously on the table. This can be illustrated by the classic nine dots problem: Try to connect these nine dots with only four straight lines.

As everyone now knows, the only way to do so is to mentally go outside the frame created by the nine dots:

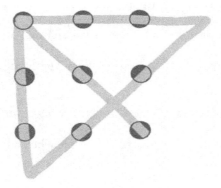

The sensei's role is to get managers to look up from their immediate delivery focus and see what other aspects of the situation, currently outside the scope, either in the larger picture or the smaller detail, can hold the key to the solution.

A gemba walk makes the company more competitive by 1/ clarifying a deeper understanding of the challenges it faces and 2/ intensifying the collaboration, both from top to bottom, between executives and employees, and also across functions.

The aim of a gemba walk is not to find solutions or take immediate actions but to clarify a shared understanding of the problems we all face together. This involves:

1. *Observation* of specific issues where things don't go as intended, listening to the people who *do* the value-adding work experience.

2. *Discussion* of what these issues mean both in the details of operations but also at strategic level for the company on its markets, with its customers, competitors and supplier networks.

3. *Commitment* to problem solve in order to investigate further—not to fix the issue but take the time to have a research project so that everyone understands much better what is going on. The assumption is that if people understand better what they do, they perform better at every aspect of their job.

The *output* of a gemba walk should be a learning project that will enrich everyone's understanding of their job—from operator to CEO. A *good* output is when the sensei strikes gold and finds a learning project that will lead to a transformative experience. For instance, in one company, fixing the spare parts supply for maintenance operations eventually led to creating a spare parts supply platform for the entire industry (competitors purchase their own spare parts through the platform because its faster than through internal channels) which radically changed the competitive positioning of the firm. This opened up the "digital" debate and led the company to develop an app for its customer service and accidentally acquire the capability to help its own customers with data analysis—a service that customers jumped on immediately. Although the sensei had very little idea about the digital revolution, he understood its importance and challenged the company to become the "amazon of spare parts." The company's own learning generated a completely new set of questions and led it to see the potential of a total digital transformation (in particular in dealing with subcontractors to handle demand variability) in a sector where it seemed remote and unlikely.

The main tool of sensei-ing is "helicopter thinking"—starting the discussion on a very detailed operational point (often where things don't go as they're supposed to) and then ascending to the big picture, seeing the strategic implications of what is being looked at—and returning to the ground. Sensei are only as good as their ability to observe in both the minutest detail (looking for "one second of waste"); as well as being able to sense at the strategic business level (which was kind of obvious for people steeped in their industry as the original sensei were, but is by no means obvious).

A good sensei reliably finds transformative experiences for people to grow—and accompanies them in facing the obstacles they encounter. This, however, is far from easy or simple. Sensei-ing faces (at least) five difficult problems which can only be resolved if would-be sensei practice their own self-study exercises:

1. *Pick the right challenge:* Workplaces are complex and confusing, and everyone is used to things as they are. The sensei needs to find and point to the right concrete problems to make strategic points.

2. *Make the challenge relevant to executives:* The orientation power of senior executives is inescapable—their attitude is the prime factor that will make the gemba walk a success or not. The sensei needs to keep the visit relevant to executives and keep them interested and open.

3. *Challenge in a productive yet safe manner:* Gemba walks are by design socially awkward, as pointing out problems in front of both the hierarchy and the frontline workers makes everyone defensive: CEOs fear not having answers, operators fear what will happen to them if they tell the truth, middle-managers fear everything and are systematically defensive. The sensei needs to create a safe place for everyone to feel they've learned something useful and problems can be resolved.

4. *Ask open questions that can lead to concrete improvements:* To explore topics they don't have answers to, managers need both motivation and space to think—if the problem feels too difficult or too distant from day to day context, it will just be ignored. If too familiar, it will be treated as routine. The sensei needs to express a concrete problem which will help teams develop without feeling out of reach, and then push for the next step.

5. *Make it visible:* The better the visual management, the easier everyone recognizes problems. In order to avoid being seen as only a critic, but as someone who will contribute, the sensei needs to contribute firsthand to the workplace by making visual management improvement suggestions.

None of these core problems are simple, and because of the highly social and emotional nature of the gemba walk situation, one never gets it quite right: too tight and people are upset and close their minds, too loose and they don't see it as relevant and dismiss it. The commitment to learning by doing, however, remains central. As the legendary Art Byrne's own sensei used to repeat "if you don't try something, no knowledge can visit you."

Being credible on the gemba, to both senior executives and frontline associates, is not an easy challenge. Is there a secret sauce to sensei-ing? Something you really need to know to get started? No more than the secret to be a great teacher—remain a learner.

The secret to being a lean sensei is the same as to being a great teacher—explore your own research topics, before trying to convince others to do the same. Beyond understanding lean tools and principles, the sensei needs to handle the gemba situation that brings together, at the work place, senior executives, middle managers and value-adding associates. Our social organizations are designed to keep these people in separate worlds and a successful gemba walk hinges on knowing how to create teamwork from asking *good questions*, with a *good attitude,* to spur collective learning. What type of personal research topics should a sensei set himself or herself? To become a *better* sensei?

# 6

# FIVE KEY SENSEI-ING QUESTIONS TO REMAIN A LEARNER

The obvious starting point to sensei-ing is constantly referring back to the basics of the TPS and the other aspects of the Toyota Way. What do the terms mean in different contexts? How do steps (such as 1/ pull logistics to clear the window, 2/ better detect quality problems to solve them right away, 3/ ask every person to check their own procedures for standards to uphold, 4/ support each and every one in a waste elimination improvement project, 5/ apply in the current conditions? The TPS is the basic gemba of sensei, and its understanding can be deepened every day, everywhere.

The deeper topic of meditation for a sensei is first, understanding the evolution of customer preferences according to changes in lifestyle (value), second, the resolution of problems on products currently in production (value analysis) which leads to, third, the understanding of what needs to be improved at the engineering stage (value engineering) and thus (fourth) where investment is needed in fundamental capabilities and know-how for innovation. As a sensei, it's important to accept that each of these topics are just as challenging to you as they are to the people you're trying to help. Acknowledging this (as opposed to setting yourself up as a superior "knower") is the key to creating the conditions for a shared experience of learning together by fully sharing the responsibility of the problems faced.

To improve, gemba walk after gemba walk, sensei must learn just as they teach. There are a few skills specific to sensei-ing on which we can expect high standards and which can be improved through deliberate practice, and, in process, forming one's own style.

## 1. RECOGNIZING THE DEEPER SYNDROME BY ITS SIGNS AND SYMPTOMS

Sensei look for teachable problems—concrete issues that will turn out to be strategic to the company. The sensei's job is to transform a vague issue into a clear problem, expressed as a gap to a standard. Since sensei don't have a crystal ball, a key part of the role is recognizing signs of deeper problems.

To investigate an issue, you've got to start somewhere. This is not an open-eye exercise, this is mentally manipulating a situation until you see an issue. Helicopter thinking is all about viewing the situation from the top, and then descending into the fine details of the work.

From the top, this mostly involves understanding how the business makes money. You can't go wrong in asking yourself: Who are their customers? What is the average basket size worth? How do they make any money by:

How do they cover for their asset costs ➔ by how people satisfy customers and at what cost ➔ by how they use materials and partners.

For example, if you sit in a café which is largely empty at this time of the day and where a couple of waiters are chatting to each other rather than coming over to ask if you want something else, you can make the safe hypothesis that the wine in your glass is vastly overpriced. The only way to compensate for poor asset productivity and poor labor productivity has to be materials productivity. This is not a conclusion, it's a starting place. (Of course, don't do this at home, because this will start you thinking on the quality of the wine, then comparing it to what nice wine should taste like—your standard—and end up generally disappointed).

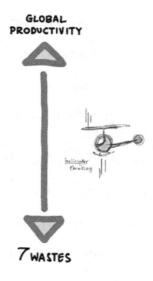

Taiichi Ohno is quoted saying: "there is a secret to the shop floor just as there is a secret to a magic trick. Let me tell you what it is. To get rid of muda you have to cultivate the ability to see muda. And you have to think about how to get rid of the muda you've seen. You repeat this—always, everywhere, tirelessly and relentlessly."[17]

The well-known seven wastes are typical symptoms of deeper

---

17    Hino, S., 2006, Inside The Mind of Toyota, Productivity Press, New York.

issues, in any circumstances. They orient your eyes to look into any activity from Ohno's perspective. They educate you to see the details of any process. They invariably reveal deeper underlying problems that are calling out to be addressed.

- *Overproduction reveals a lack of flexibility:* producing more than customer demand is the result of batching work. We batch because it's more convenient as it's often hard to shift from one type of work to another. Executives think it perfectly normal and sensible to 1/ group demand to make machines work at full capacity and 2/ place demand where work is the cheapest. This creates unnecessary batches, which are then spread out geographically, and means that each segment works ahead of real customer demand. Inventories accumulate, sometimes containing defective or out-of-date parts.

- *Defectives are a symptom of lack of engineering understanding of the materials, the components and the process:* delivering defects or correcting comes from gaps in the understanding of the steps to produce good work. Very often, it means that some parameter is too close to a practical limit and random events push the process over the limit, creating a defect. Looking into defectives will reveal gaps in fundamental understanding of product design or process design.

- *Waiting is a symptom of stop-and-go and lack of understanding of takt time:* many operations look like grandad's army—run, wait, run, wait—such stop and go is a symptoms of authority gates (only go to the next step when I authorize it) and batching (then move as a group all at once) which, in itself reflects the lack of takt time. When takt time is clear, no organization is needed because people all know when to deliver what, and self-organize to do what needs to be done. Waiting reveals the syndrome that some boss controls who does what where, on his or her say-so, irrespective of customer demand.

- *Transporting reveals the holding of large inventories organized by specialty:* in any typical process, work is broken down into different tasks, which are then carried out in specialized centers. Work-in-progress products have to be moved from one area to the next, or service files have to move from one desk to the next. The text you are reading has to be moved between its various authors, and then to the editors' desk, then approved by the publisher, then to the copy-editor's desk, then back to the authors and so on. Because such transport is hassle, things are moved in batches to minimize their cost. Even in the case of something immaterial, as a word file, the instinct is to wait until all work is finished at one stage until moving it to the next because it's simpler to organize.

- *Movement indicates lack of ownership by the operators of their own workplace:* "foot movement, hand movement, eye move-ment," is one of the first thing you're taught to look at in lean, because it reflects a work environment not designed to make standard work cycles smooth and seamless, the way people would have organized their workplace if they felt ownership and responsibility.

- *Over-processing is a symptom of lack of understanding of what is critical to quality:* it's one thing to learn to play a piece of music, it's another one entirely to learn to make it swing. Without understanding the subtle things that make the difference between work and good work, the risk is to over-work some aspects and ignore others more important—thus creating unnecessary work in terms of correcting defectives. Overprocessing means paying too much attention to things that don't matter to the final product and run the risk of missing what really makes quality—a common occurrence in bureaucratic environments where formal quality control outweighs the spirit of quality.

- *Inventory on hand signals a lack of understanding of the importance of relationship with suppliers:* we keep more components on hand because we don't trust suppliers to deliver quickly what we need when we need it—these components then need to be stored and their accumulation skews the real demand to customers since the rule followed is **Demand = Real Demand - Stock on hand + Safety Stock,** a failproof recipe to create huge *mura* (demand variation), *muri* by overburdening the supplier with sudden peaks of demand and thus *muda* in inventory.

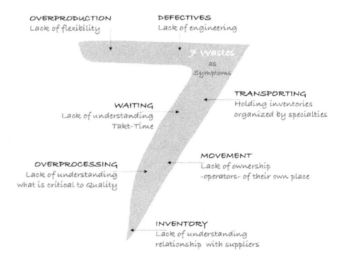

OVERPRODUCTION
Lack of flexibility

DEFECTIVES
Lack of engineering

7 Wastes
as
Symptoms

TRANSPORTING
Holding inventories
organized by specialties

WAITING
Lack of understanding
Takt-Time

MOVEMENT
Lack of ownership
-operators- of their own place

OVERPROCESSING
Lack of understanding
what is critical to Quality

INVENTORY
Lack of understanding
relationship with suppliers

Each of these seven wastes are symptoms of practices that seem perfectly normal to financial managers, but create poor performance at the overall system level—which most managers in bureaucratized, specialized and Taylorized companies will never see.

A "good" issue is a problem, often a waste, that originates with something everyone expects is normal—and even right. For instance, 1% defects in any process produces 10,000 bad parts per million and the symptom that at least one product or process engineering constraint is not fully understood. Everyone in the company agrees that 1) in one process we are too close to physical tolerances but we (and no one else) don't know how to do things better, 2) so natural variability makes occasional defects which we inspect out, and 3) a few will make it through the process to the customer, but that's an unavoidable cost of doing business.

A core insight of lean is that main costs are common to every business, such as the cost of equipment, the cost of hiring people locally, the cost of purchasing materials on markets, but that competitiveness can be sought in the layer of unnecessary costs created by our misconceptions—erroneous beliefs that lead us to work poorly with people, assets and materials and thus create waste.

Wrong-headed thinking occurs when people are persuaded that something is perfectly normal and right, and it turns out to be a wrong, costly notion. When people see the mistakes in their thinking, they tend to correct themselves and mend the errors of their ways. Thinking, however, is rather sticky and if an error is commonly shared, it's hard to get people to see it.

To grasp the learning problem, we first need to understand why no one sees it at as a problem. Humans, usually, act to correct what they see as an issue. But in many cases, they also get used to dysfunctional, toxic or plainly crazy situations simply because they don't relate a common symptom (say, fuel consumption from driving your car or taking a plane) to a global problem (man-made climate change). Habituation, erasing from consciousness low intensity frequent signals, ensures that human beings get used to almost anything, regardless of how crazy it looks from the outside. The job of the sensei is to look beyond *signs*—the fact that something in front of your very eyes doesn't look right—to *symptoms*, a sign that repeats itself and might signal a deeper, more structural issues, to *syndromes*, commonly held misconceptions.

A syndrome is a shared idea that everyone thinks is natural, right and even good when in fact it's a mistake. A syndrome is believing that there is a natural cost of quality in doing business and that it's not worth the effort figuring out the origin since we're already doing what we can—it would be too expensive to fix. Another one is thinking there is no point in training people since they eventually leave. (Executive: "what if I train people and they leave?" Sensei: "what if you don't and they stay?")

As a sensei, you're no more clairvoyant than anybody else, but you can practice daily your understanding of syndromes:

- *Signs:* something is not right, or not what is expected.

- *Symptoms:* some signs are symptoms, they show up all over the place in different ways but they point out to something we do that generates them.

- *Syndromes:* false beliefs that everyone believes are 1) natural and 2) good that generate the symptoms.

Typical syndromes would be "of course we carry inventory, suppliers never deliver on time," or, "of course we have 100% inspection to spot defectives, this engineering tolerance is impossible to hold," "Let's automate rather than train people", "let's fudge the figures to get the tender, we'll negotiate with customers after they've signed" and so on.

The sensei's number one skill is to distinguish dumb issues—something went wrong that day for no particular reason, it will be fixed and won't happen again—with ignorance issues—there is a commonly held false belief that generates this problem everywhere, every day, in different forms. Making a big case of a dumb issue is a waste of time for everyone and a loss of credibility as a sensei. Insisting on an issue that no one thinks is a problem and later will turn out as strategic is what makes a legendary sensei.

To practice sensei skills, the first self-development project is to continuously challenge your own ability to distinguish dumb issues from deep syndromes.

## 2.  LEARNING THE CEO LANGUAGE OF SHAREHOLDER VALUE

A sure test of a successful gemba walk is the scheduling of the next one—this might sound trivial, but dealing with senior executives and business leaders, it never is. Their time is measured and if they don't see value in something, they simply don't do it. They promise they will and reschedule, something else has come up, etc. A clear sign the lean effort is flagging is having gemba walks postponed. CEOs and COOs must find each gemba walk both interesting and worthwhile.

What do CEOs talk about when they meet each other? Essentially, two things: valuation and people—hiring, firing and promotion.

Valuation is the language of the senior executive world, from which almost all others are excluded by the very nature of the activity. Valuation is how CEOs are judged and even if they don't necessarily appraise themselves that way they can't escape it (many CEOs do think about long term growth, customer satisfaction, employee morale and technology choices, but then their investors only look at the spot share price). Valuation is how shareholders and other financial players, such as funds and banks estimate the *value* of the company—and so the value of its CEO.

At its simplest, the value of a company derives from the cash flow it generates. For instance, if I purchase a company at five times its EBITDA, I'm hoping it will pay for itself in five years. But then what if the company has a lot of cash in its bank accounts—surely you should add this to its value? And what about its assets? The company can always be broken up and the sum of the assets sold independently might be more than the profit returns of the whole? And what if its sales are growing rapidly? Or slowing down?

The basic valuation theory is:

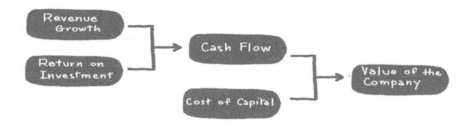

But in practice, anything goes. Acquirers can value a company on the basis of its market size to complement their strategy. The value will then be a multiple of the firm's turnover. Or they can value it from its stock market value. Or because they really, really want it.

In any case, the value of the company will be an alchemical formula involving its sales growth (or decline), the free cash flow it generates, its assets and equity, its access to capital and how markets and shareholders feel on the day.

While this is very far from any sensei's world, it's what CEOs live with every day. There are clear connections:

- Quality of current products ➜ current sales

- New products in development ➜ future sales

- Productivity of labor and materials ➜ current cash flow

- Productivity of assets (and inventory rotation) ➜ future cash flow

But the language is completely different. Would-be sensei can't limit themselves purely to operational matters. They are not expected to master the finer points of finance, leveraging, valuation and so on, but they need to recognize the language and learn enough of it not to be completely at sea when these debates do come up.

To keep a senior executive interested in the workplace and keep her coming back to the coal face listening to the people doing the value-adding work, sensei need to constantly hone their skill of translating what they see into the CEO language of shareholder value—the impact it has at financial and organizational level—and continue to argue for long term value creation, not just for shareholder, but for customers, employees and society at large as well.

The oldest sensei story we've heard dates to the eighties when a global electronics manufacturer had just completed a leading-edge automated warehouse. Having heard that these Toyota guys were very good at logistics, they invited a delegation to visit the new, fully automatic installation. Throughout the visit the Japanese visitors were openly appreciative and admirative of all the automated devices they were shown, guaranteeing their host they had nothing like that at Toyota. By the end of the tour, the electronics managers were feeling comforted and pleased with themselves, when they were asked a final question: "why have a warehouse at all?"

This story sounds like a typical cryptic old-time sensei anecdote, until we translate it in a debate over investment on technology (the automation) versus the productivity of assets and the cash flow sunk into the inventory held in the warehouse. The question here is whether the firm's valuation is improved by adding the automated warehouse and the inventory it holds to the books (the balance sheet looks better, and any hope of replacing humans by machines always sounds good to financiers) or, on the contrary, whether the company's valuation is reduced by sinking cash flow and investments into unnecessary inventory and the costs of inventory management—no matter how automated.

The second topic that CEOs obsess with is hiring and firing—or promoting. CEOs accept that talent at executive level is the key to their success, but they tend to think in bureaucratic terms:

- *Hiring a person to fit a role:* the CEO draws the organization and defines the scope of the role and its connections in the organizational chart, and looks for someone to fit the box.

- *People find personal fulfillment within the strategy:* CEOs are endlessly surprised that the people they hire don't simply do what they're asked but, instead, bring their own agendas and do their own things.

The moment senior executives get involved, any conversation turns political. The sensei wades in a world of who's in favor and who's out, who is allied with whom and who hates whose guts. There is no way to get involved at CEO level and somehow stay clear of corporate politics.

In this context, the sensei's role is to bring gemba realities into the discussion. "Fact is fact," used to repeat one of our sensei. What can't be ignored is that "facts" will help some executives with their own agenda, and hinder others—so reactions can be unexpected. Furthermore, CEOs are constantly thinking in terms of who they want to promote and who they want to replace—whether they act on it or not. Sensei need to realize they're involved, like it or not, because learning the language of CEOs essentially means discussing *people*: what they get, what they don't get, and what their personal agendas are relative to what the CEO is trying to do.

Sensei are rarely top management material—their interests lie elsewhere and the main reason they become sensei is that they want the world to make sense and help others develop and progress. Would-be sensei will be equally uncomfortable with the valuation and people discussions. A core tenet of sensei-ing is "ask 'why?,' not 'who?'". Yet, to be successful at gemba walks, one cannot ignore that valuation calculations are always there in the background and that CEOs tend to think in terms of "who shall I ask whom to do what? And will they do it?" Fact is fact, and keeping senior leaders interested in gemba walks involves learning to speak their language and understanding their worldview.

### 3. CREATE A SAFE SPACE FOR DISCUSSION AND REFLECTION

Listen until it hurts! Gemba walks are tough on executives, but they're even harder on operators themselves. From the operator's point of view, here comes a posse of very senior people suddenly looking at them like bugs under a magnifying glass and asking foolish questions.

Gemba walks are socially awkward. Executives rarely introduce themselves assuming everyone knows who they are, and barely take the time to say hello. Operators tend to stare like deer caught in the headlights or hunker down on their work and ignore everyone altogether. Middle-managers sweat through it justifying everything and jumping in between the execs and what there is to see.

Because of these unavoidable asymmetries, the challenge of a gemba walk is to keep discussions to a minimum—and to manage the discussion space. The best way to do this is to have prepared kaizen presentations where teams explain the gain they were after, the problem they tried to resolve, how they went about it, how it worked out and what support they need. Creating a formal, safe space, makes it much easier to discuss issues.

"Look, listen, smell," was the advice of an old-time sensei at Honda. Presence is the main tool of the sensei—focus—hearing what people are actually saying, literally. Looking at what they are doing that varies with what they are saying. Looking for what is *not there* as well as what they show you. The strength of equal attention to everyone, from operator to CEO is what creates the unique gemba walk experience of respect for people: making the fullest effort to understand each other's point of view—especially when it is difficult and emotionally charged.

What sensei really bring to the gemba is their *way to see.* By looking at this or that, the sensei draws attention and usually uncovers waste. The ability to command this attention through sheer presence is essential to successful sensei-ing. As you walk with executives on middle-managers turf, expect to face:

- *Validation:* tell me that what we're doing is OK.

- *Justification:* yes, some things are not great, but, listen, here is why we have no choice but do it this way.

- *Rationalization:* although the way we go about things might seem wrong to you, it's really good because of this or that side benefit—walking on your hands saves the use on your shoes.

The difficulty lies in simultaneously listening, and proving that you do, without accepting the terms or the logic of the person who is, quite legitimately, defending their way of running things. A large part of the sensei's presence lies in her ability not to get distracted by the discourse but keep focused on what is there to be seen (funnily, managers will often stand right in front of you, to block you from looking further into what you're looking at) and bring other's attention to *learn to see.* It's hard to get right the Yin-Yang balance of listening/challenging, and something sensei constantly try to improve.

Nampachi Hayashi, one of Toyota's legendary sensei recommends to "use feet, hands and parts to see the true facts by going and seeing for yourself":

- Don't look with your eyes, look with your feet

- Don't think with your head, think with your hands

- Don't ask the person, ask the parts

This advice sounds easy to dismiss as Toyota folklore, but it really is at the heart of developing the sensei presence on the gemba: not getting distracted by arguments but following the trail by going and looking (look with your feet) and thinking concretely rather than getting carried away by "in theory" arguments (think with your hands) and follow what really happens to work (ask the parts).

Sensei need to learn to steer the discussion away from face-to-face confrontations and get the gemba walk group to actually look at what is going on, without discussing too much with frontline staff beyond courtesies. Operators speak volumes in the way they work, but when asked for their opinion in front of senior hierarchy, feel very uneasy—and can react oddly.

A gemba walk is successful if frontline people feel proud of what they've shown and if senior managers feel they've uncovered something interesting which they didn't know before. In an unsuccessful gemba walk, people on the ground feel dismissed or despised and the senior people feel they haven't learned anything useful. Climbing to the top of the mountain is hard, rolling down the hill is easy, particularly in difficult company cultures. Much of the success of a gemba walk depends on the sensei's ability to keep the group's attention focused on what happens and not who's at fault. Maintaining both "problems first," and "not guilty" requires savvy, and needs constant practice.

## 4. CHOOSING NEXT STEP DEVELOPMENTAL PROBLEMS

The idea that gemba walks by top managers can build greater organizational effectiveness rests on three fundamental assumptions:

1. If people better understand what they do, they perform better.

2. To help people enrich their understanding of what they do, get them to practice solving specific problems, which will deepen their thinking, and offer opportunities for insight and initiative.

3. Few organizational problems can be solved on one's own, and encouraging people to solve problems together, whether as a team or across functional boundaries is the key to both enlarging their worldview and developing their influence in the company.

These assumptions are hard to dispute on the face of it, but they have a serious flaw: what does "understand" really mean? As in any classroom, in a gemba walk, people will quickly encounter facts and procedures (steps to do things). As in any classroom to actually learn something, they need *meaning*.

Meaning is that special feeling we get when we connect the dots. New facts and procedures enrich our understanding when we can connect them to the network of facts and procedures we already know. Sometimes we get an "aha!" moment when a previously unconnected dot suddenly connects and our understanding pivots around that new connection—"ah! I see! From this perspective it all looks different." But conversely, in many cases new facts or frameworks simply don't connect and remain… meaningless.

What do you see here?

Some of you will see the young woman (well, now we've said it, all of you);

Some of you will have seen the old woman (well, now we've said it, all of you);

Some of you will see how the illusion is produced (well, now that we've said it, all of you).

In ambiguous situations, such as this cartoon, the way questions are framed (young? old? illusion?) largely determines how cues and context are interpreted. Problem solving helps people to go beyond jumping to a solution or an opinion, the reaction of memory, and learn to truly think by manipulating objects mentally until they see them from different angles and perspectives.

Problem-solving is more powerful than just explaining or lecturing because it gets people to engage with new facts, and look for meaning on their own. If they embrace the problem, they will find out new things and connect them—deepening their understanding.

However, if the problem feels too remote to the present situation, or too unconnected to the current context, people will shrug it off, pay lip service if they have to, but not really try and therefore not learn much. This was a frequent problem in the old days when learning from the original sensei—the challenges they gave seemed obvious to them, but strange and arbitrary to the recipients, who would mostly dismiss the question hoping it would go away. And, to be fair, this happens to this very day during gemba walks, especially in the beginning phase.

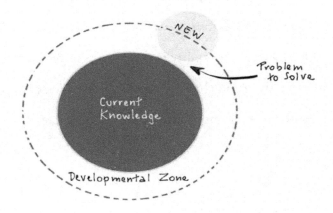

To support people in their development, sensei have to learn to give challenging, concrete problems which people also accept as relevant and valid in their current context. This is rarely obvious because of two mental biases:

- It's very hard to imagine that others don't know what we know and to represent what they do know and start from there.

- We assume we use the same terms in the same way but that's rarely the case as the same word can mean very different things to different people.

A sensei's job is to point to problems, discuss ideals and sketch a way to look for answers without ever giving a specific solution. This hinges on the ability to pick the right problems, which will be interesting and challenging enough to prick curiosity, but not so outlandish or impossible looking that people dismiss them—a hard balance to find.

## 5.  DEVELOPING VISUAL MANAGEMENT

In the lean tradition, sensei also contribute directly to the work-place through "visual management"—finding ways to visualize work processes so that work appears more intuitive in terms of output goals and sequences of steps, and so that problems are revealed at first glance.

In the West, visual management is often interpreted by middle-managers as posting PowerPoint slides on the walls so that people see how they're monitored and action plans can be tracked visibly. Managers have also adopted post-it notes as a way to formalize issues and manage the importance/urgency priority conflicts.

This has little to do with visual management as it was originally intended. Real visual management is closer to the visual traffic system that allows you to find where to return a rental car at an unfamiliar airport without too much trouble. Sometimes the signs are very intuitive, sometimes it feels they have been designed specifically to get you lost.

30 to 50% of our brain matter is dedicated to vision (as opposed to 10% to touch, and 3% to hearing). Any visual information is processed seamlessly and unconsciously, and will trump any oral information at every turn. Visual management techniques are close to choice-engineering: giving visual cues of what needs to happen when so that people make intuitively the right choices without having to think about it or to be told what to do.

Much of visual management has to do with clarifying the logistics of work so that both the pace of output and the flow of components (whether material or informational) is as clear as can be and hiccups appear as quickly as possible, as opposed to being hidden in stocks or backlogs—lists.

This specific skill is inherent in the lean tradition, and, in order to be able to transform issues into problems, a sensei needs to convince people to implement visual management practices to make concrete thinking easier by measuring actual against planned.

As Takehiko Harada explains, kaizen is really about *moving value closer to the final customer.* This general principle orients the kind of exercise a sensei is looking for. The skill lies in proposing the right challenge on the gemba according to the five previous disciplines so that it *makes sense* to the CEO and team members alike. A good sensei shows the leader how to create the conditions for kaizen: how to challenge and support front-line teams so that they experiment with kaizen and see the benefits of kaizen, so that they keep practicing it and develop their own kaizen spirit. Of course, as leaders work with a sensei's suggestions for improving visual management to make work more intuitive and reveal problems, the production system itself evolves step by step. If we want to practice what we preach, we need, as sensei, to have an idea of our own "True North"—the ideal conditions we're seeking for an education system overlaying the production system. What would that look like?

# 7

# LEAN AS AN EDUCATION SYSTEM, TO IMPROVE THE PRODUCTION SYSTEM

Toyota turned to learning and education to gain the upper hand on its market through a large, frequently renewed line-up, high quality and cost effectiveness. The architect of the Toyota we know today was Eiji Toyoda (1913—2013), who led the company in its heyday (he was also the driving force behind the Prius hybrid car challenge to drastically lower automobile consumption and emissions). He built on breakthrough ideas of his uncle, Sakichi Toyoda, the inventor of "intelligent automation," and his cousin, Kiichiro Toyoda, who conceived "just-in-time," to fully systematize the education system. His own personal contribution to the edifice was the suggestions program he discovered while visiting Ford in the 1950s, and which became the bedrock of "good thinking, good products."

All these various ideas came together as an operational system as the company grew rapidly. Its leadership faced the unpalatable fact that progress in quality was not keeping pace with increases in productivity. Too many new workers, not enough training, lack of cross-functional communication, and all the usual symptoms of Big Company Disease. Eiji Toyoda, then an executive Vice-President, was tasked with consolidating all TQC activities, from product planning through to design, production and sales, and ended up building the foundational learning systems that would propel Toyota to world market dominance.

As a way to turn its commitment to "quality first" into a concrete challenge for the whole company, Toyota pursued the Deming Prize, which it was awarded in 1965. The prize was established in 1951 to honor Dr. Deming's contribution to Japanese industry's fast advances in quality improvement. In this we can consider Deming as the sensei of all sensei, as few people's words have had such as profound impact on industry (as Taiichi Ohno also had with *kanban* and *kaizen*). To understand how Toyota shaped its response to its quality challenge, we can delve further into Deming's own thinking. He believed that the road to transformation rested upon *Profound Knowledge*. A system of profound knowledge, he thought, should be composed of four parts, all related to each other:

- Appreciation for a system

- Knowledge about variation

- Theory of knowledge

- Psychology[18]

We believe that Toyota did just that: develop a system of profound knowledge by seeing the firm as a system, understanding the impact of mura, muri, muda, developing its own theory of knowledge and of people development. Any theory of knowledge needs three core elements:

- *Try and see:* to try new things and explore what works and what doesn't.

- *Theory:* to derive meaning from practice and build a body of knowledge.

- *Test model:* measurements and metrics to distinguish fact from opinion.

---

18    Deming, W. E. (1994) The New Economics, MIT Press, Cambridge

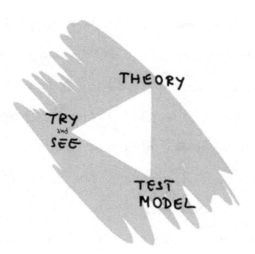

Omit any of these three components, and you get experience, or philosophy, or reporting but very little learning and actual knowledge. And exclude psychology, a theory of motivation and how people think, and you simply get good intentions with no concrete improvements. "Experience alone, without theory," Deming quipped, "teaches management nothing about what to do to improve quality and competitive position, nor how to do it."[19]

---

19   Deming, W. E. (1982) *Out Of The Crisis*, MIT, Center for Advanced Educational Services, Cambridge

We also find another set of trade-offs typical of the lean approach. In Scandinavia, one TQM sensei got so impatient with the Nordic tendency to discuss things endlessly before trying something that he told the group they were not worthy of discussing the theory until they had tried the practice. Indeed, Taiichi Ohno's introduction to the first written TPS manual is about "practice over theory."

Nonetheless, our experience with old time sensei is that they get you time and time again to state your understanding of theory before trying a change. Indeed, what we have often seen, even within Toyota, is that when the Japanese sensei leave, the plant carries on with the rituals of kaizen, but no longer seeks to clarify the theoretical level, or indeed to check rigorously results, and improvements slow down very quickly as a result. In the same text, Ohno offers interesting insight on the tension between theory and practice:

"When you try to perform such an obvious thing [just-in-time], you will collide with various problems, making it quite unfeasible. Even if ideals are like that, if we say that they are unrealistic ideals, then that is all they can be.

Considering that the character "理 (logic)" in "合理化 (rationalization)" is the same "理" from "理想 (Ideal)", for someone who is striving for rationalization, everything becomes about implementation, or a challenge about how close you can get to it.

Just in time, productivity, cost, and shifting the burden towards outsourcing; judging from common logic, all of these are thought to be full of contradictory aspects. We must break this wall of common logic and make those mutually contradictory points coexist through what we nowadays call "*logic escape.*""[20]

This "logic escape", the breaking of trade-offs through a moment of creative insight by thinking with your hands and

---

20    Toyota Handbook, 1973 edition, annotated by Mark Warren, 2018.

trying things, as well as testing your theories and measuring results is the cornerstone of Toyota's approach to psychology. Motivation comes from success, and old-time sensei think that if all people can engage in kaizen and experience good results, their motivation will increase due to the "joy of creation." The reasoning is the following:

Everyone wants to contribute ➔excess energy goes into non value-added work ➔ we need to change waste into work ➔ tasks are achieved with ease as a matter of course

With a strong kaizen spirit ➔ everyone can have good results ➔ which creates motivation ➔ and discover the joy of creation ➔ to build respect for people

The underlying theory is that people's sense of achievement draws from practicing kaizen, which itself rests on a shared understanding of problems, supporting teamwork and encouraging a kaizen mindset. This, in turn rests on full communication and employee participation.

Toyota, from which most of lean is inspired, has far more than a practice of production. It has a clear business and product theory that guides its production practices. It has its own psychology theory that guide its management practices. The causes for its enduring success, with leading market share and the profitability of a luxury boutique, as well as innovative green products, are found not just in its TPS but its approach to long-term profitability as a whole and its system to develop better cars, model after model.

For some bizarre reason, the business world has decided it can progress through practice alone, as reflected by the current obsession with "best practices." As we now know, real learning occurs through Plan-Do-Check-Act, which means concrete changes to our current theory with a measurable impact. In the lean approach, the sensei's contribution is to create the conditions for PDCA by everyone everywhere all the time, which, unavoidably, means that we need to build our own theory of sensei-ing.[21]

---

21    The PDCA cycle as drawn by W. Edwards Deming from Walter Shewhart's dynamic scientific process of acquiring knowledge in H. Neave, (1990) *The Deming Dimension*, SPC Press, Knoxville.

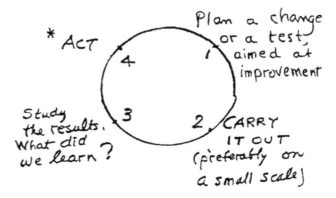

THE SHEWHART CYCLE

* ACT

4

1  Plan a change
or a test,
aimed at
improvement

3  Study
the results.
What did
we learn?

2  CARRY
IT OUT
(preferably on
a small scale)

* ACT.  Adopt the change.
or  Abandon it.
or  Run through the cycle
again, possibly under
different environmental
conditions.

22

---

22   "The Deming Dimension," by Henry R. Neave. © 1990 Henry R. Neave. Published by
SPC Press, Knoxville, Tennessee, USA. All Rights Reserved.

Lean is widely considered to be merely a production system that reduces defects mechanistically (the "understanding of variation" in Deming's thinking) while its scope goes much further. A core lean insight is to replace instructions with challenges and problem solving, in order to educate people rather than control them.

If it is an education system that creates the conditions for continuous improvement by continuously developing people, who educates the educators? The first generation of lean practitioners learned the tradition from their sensei. By practicing the same exercises in various situations, the pioneers progressively developed their own intuitive grasp of the principles: customer satisfaction, jidoka, just-in-time, heijunka, standardized work, kaizen, basic stability. Mastering these principles doesn't mean setting the right production methods, but offering learning experiences to the next generation of lean practitioners.

No one knows what tomorrow is going to be like, let alone five years from now: it's impossible to simply acquire and apply the "best practices" of the future—these are not known yet. Any best practices around are there to make you *run-of-the-mill*, since everyone does the same thing. They won't make you competitive.

To keep performing, there is no other known way than to keep discovering. This means constantly focusing on the next step, *without knowing in advance what it will be.* The lean system is a way to systematically define next steps in order to experiment with everyone, everywhere, all the time.

Recent research in organizational studies shows conclusively that performance is linked to the *flow of ideas*—how new ideas are generated and flow through the organization, from one person to the next. As serial entrepreneur and MIT Professor Alex Pentland puts it: "The rate of idea flow is a critical measure of how the social network functions in collecting and refining decision strategies… the rate of idea flow can also be used to predict productivity and creative output."[23] Many successful companies

---

23    Pentland, A. (2014) Social Physics, The Penguin Press, New York.

have understood this over the years, and found ad-hoc ways to increase the flow of ideas. Toyota is the first to have systematized doing so with specific support tools, such as suggestions system, self-study and quality circles activities and Hoshin Kanri. Sensei have a key role in developing the education system that supports the flow of ideas—but are by no means the whole story.

The sensei role is a Western invention, much like consultant or coach. What we have seen in Toyota is a learning organization with various roles at various levels:

| Role | Level | To develop |
|------|-------|------------|
| Sensei | Executive | Challenge and gemba leadership |
| Lean officer | Manager | Kaizen and self-study activities |
| Trainer | Team member | Skills and on the job development |

These are not organizational roles. The aim is to have a *research* project at each level. The CEO and the sensei need many research projects to see and learn. Middle managers sometimes need a helping hand to carry out research projects, whether from an external consultant or lean officer. At any level of skill, we all need a trainer to teach us the next level of proficiency. These various aspects need not be organized, but can be, and within Toyota we have seen many different ways of doing so, from Japanese coordinators doubling as managers, to kaizen offices in which line managers are seconded to prepare them for their next promotion and so on. There is no "best practice." The role of the CEO is to understand the need for an education system, and to build his or her own as best she can:

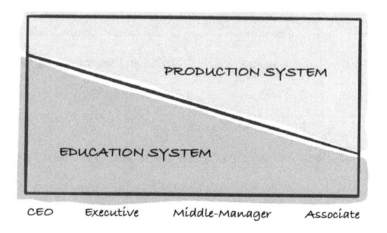

# CONCLUSION

Lean is the first, truly global management system. Lean is inspired from Toyota, who developed a management system based on what its engineers learned from German engineers, and trying to copy American engineers—adding some Japanese ingenuity. Lean is not the *Toyota Production System* nor any of the other aspects of the *Toyota Way* per se, but an attempt to generalize the performance lessons from Toyota (a disruptive green innovator with the largest market share and the profitability of a luxury boutique) outside the company, the industry, the country.

The deeper lesson we've all learned from sensei, researchers, leaders and consultants alike is to consider an alternative to the traditional command-and-control mode of Western management and explore the challenge-and-support approach of the *Toyota Way*. Lean is a system to continuously develop people. For leaders, this means asking everyone to have their own research topic, whether as problem solving, individual suggestion or part of a quality circle activity—and then to advance those who excel at it.

The big change this means for leaders is not to create extensive action plans to keep everything under control but, rather, to discuss with everyone about how they understand the problem and what their next step should be according to:

1. The competitive challenges the company faces by finding concrete problems in customer usage or how people work at the gemba.

2. The ideas we have to face these challenges, and our capacity to try new stuff and apply new technologies to face and solve today's problems.

3. Getting people on board by understanding the obstacles they face, the difficulties they encounter, and encouraging their insights and initiatives—understanding where to invest in support.

A sensei's main job is to help leaders do so and define what kind of support these next steps mean to keep the company both dynamic and people-centric.

For sensei this means accepting that they shouldn't (and can't) have all the answers, but should become experts at asking the right questions, in spotting opportunities for development, challenging the logic of current thinking, setting appropriate exercises for people to expand their vision and skills. Last but not least, making sure experiments are carried out to the rigorous end of checking impact and drawing the appropriate conclusions—in other words, to *learn*.

Sensei don't coach. They don't teach (other than visual management techniques). And they don't recommend. Sensei challenge people and foster deeper observation, discussion and commitment to learning projects. In so doing they help people discover their own solutions on their own, and grow as a result, moving from small step by step improvements to full blown innovation along the way. Because, in the end, as one old time sensei used to say "the gemba is the greatest teacher."

# ACKNOWLEDGEMENTS

We are very grateful to Jacques Chaize for his fantastic artwork and insightful comments on the text.

**Michael Ballé:** This book largely came about from a discussion with my co-teachers Catherine Chabiron and Godefroy Beauvallet and the 2018 class of the *CES Lean Management* at *Télécom Evolutions* about the differences between teaching (transmission) and sensei-ing (journeying together). I am grateful to Dan Jones who pushed us to expand from the early paper to develop the argument into a full book, and to Jacques Chaize, who read every version and gifted us with his unique designs. Takao Sakai has also helped us tremendously to see beyond the barriers of our narrow cultural view points and look over the road to glimpse Mikawa spirit.

A big thanks also to sensei Cécile Roche, Richard Kaminski, Cyril Garambois, Anne-Lise Seltzer, Aurore Xemar and all my colleagues from *Institut Lean France*. Thank you to Jean Cunningham, Tom Ehrenfeld and James Connolly at LEI for making it happen and to Eric Buehrens and Jim Womack for supporting the project. Many thanks also to Planet Lean's Roberto Priolo and René Aernoudts, whose continued support for lean research has led to this book. I am also very thankful to Toyota veterans Gilberto Kosaka, Takehiko Harada, Joe Lee and Isao Yoshino and for generously sharing their knowledge of the formative years of TPS at Toyota. Special thanks to my father,

Freddy Ballé, the original French lean sensei.

Last but not least, deepest gratitude and love to Florence, Roman and Alexandre who have the patience to live with an author.

**Nicolas Chartier:** This learning journey would never have been possible without all the great team of Aramisauto.com. Together and with the drive of our sensei, Michael Ballé, we have learned through experimentations. They have always been supportive an enthusiastic! I dedicate this work to this great team and I'm very grateful to them for their energy and will to learn.

**Pascale Coignet:** The word "lean" would have never meant anything for me without the support of Françoise De Bois. She offered me two books, *Le management Lean*, from Michael Ballé and Godefroy Beauvallet, and *The Gold Mine*, and encouraged me to join a lean class, my first steps on the lean path. During one year, I have been fortunate to learn from Michael Ballé, Godefroy Beauvallet and Catherine Chabiron (and from my awesome class-mates) and think I will never stop learning from them. I am glad to be a member of the lean community and so honored to share the cover with all my co-authors: this is just a beginning, as the lean path seems to be infinite and is continuously surprising and enlightening. Thank you all, thanks to all the people who made this possible and thanks to my beloved daughter and husband to let me follow this path with love and kindness.

**Sandrine Olivencia:** Special thanks to my friends Michael Ballé, Catherine Chabiron, Régis Medina, Richard Kaminsky and Cécile Roche for countless hours of insightful conversations and deep reflections. Also a big thank you to all my colleagues at Institut Lean France who are so very active in the lean community. My deepest gratitude to my husband, Benjamin, and daughter, Emma, for their continued support and patience over the years as I experimented with lean. Thank you for being my sounding board, and sometimes even my Guinea pigs. In the end, you guys have been my true sensei.

**Daryl Powell:** Without the shared experiences and support from the following awesome people, I would never have discovered what I needed to learn to begin studying the path of the lean sensei: Bjørn Jalving, Kjell Gjestad, Stian Johansen and all of my colleagues at Kongsberg Maritime; Monica Rolfsen, Heidi Dreyer, Jonas Ingvaldsen, Marte Daae-Qvale Holmemo, Erlend Alfnes, Jan Ola Strandhagen and colleagues at the Norwegian University of Science and Technology (NTNU); my Lean Companion Torbjørn Netland at ETH Zurich; Paul Coughlan at Trinity College Dublin; Monica Rossi at Politecnico di Milano; Ottar Henriksen, Viggo Johannessen, and my other friends at Lean Forum Norge; Kjell Sigve Kvalavåg, Knut Sandbakken, and Conny Svensson at Sintef Manufacturing; Dan Jones at Lean Enterprise Academy; Jim Womack and John Shook at Lean Enterprise Institute; and of course Takao Sakai—thanks for the enlightenment at Kamakura! A special mention also to David Leese, Emrah Arica, Børge Sjøbakk, Gaute Knutstad, Erik Gran, and Sören Themann. Finally, thanks to my fellow co-authors, my mum and dad, and my family—Karen, Rebekah, Ffion and Eva.

**Eivind Reke:** I would like to extend my thanks and gratitude to the following people for all the great conversations and gemba experiences we have shared. Bjarne Berg Wig for introducing me to lean the right way. Jonathan Reams and John Richard Hanssen. Karl-Frederik Pantke, Bjørn Øgaard and Leandro Dos Santos. Marcin Gaarden and Per Kristian Strand, and the board of Los Norge: Einar, Lena, Sofie, Birgit, Anne, Alireza and Torodd. I would also like to thank my fellow co-authors. My mom and dad, and finally my family Åsne, Solvor and Tuva. Thank you all for sharing the ride.

CPSIA information can be obtained
at www.ICGtesting.com
Printed in the USA
LVHW082357200519
618553LV00031B/1029/P